F.I.R.E.

Financial Independence, Retire Early — A Practical Guide to Escaping the 9–5

Ryan Bitstone

TABLE OF CONTENTS

ISBN: 9781807650827

Published by TPSA Publishing

Introduction

I started my first business out of desperation. I started my second business from inspiration. Both have been very successful and highly profitable. And they've allowed me to live a lifestyle I absolutely enjoy while doing work I really love.

Why am I telling you this? Because I am no different than you. I'm not smarter, more talented, or luckier and I bet I don't work any harder than you do. I'm not even sure I'm a natural entrepreneur. But I knew for sure that I would never get the satisfaction and financial rewards I wanted by working in some dead-end job.

I wanted to be on FIRE: financially independent and retiring early.

And after I got there, I wanted to help other people get on FIRE. I wanted other people to realize that doing the work you love while making the income you want is not just some pipe dream. I now this from my own experience and now from seeing the success of the people I coach and train. It can happen for you, too.

> "I wanted to be on FIRE: financially independent and retiring early"

I'm going to share with you the keys to making this happen. I'm going to share some stories about the successes of others who have used these keys. I'm going to share some of the big hairy mistakes I've made along the way so you don't have to make them. I'm also going to give you some exercises to do that will get you on your way to being on FIRE.

If you've still got some doubts, that's okay. I don't know anyone who is totally confident about everything, especially starting something new. But by the end of this book, I hope you'll feel inspired and know that being on FIRE is totally within your reach.

The book itself is really in three parts. The first three chapters explore what you need to know about *yourself* before you even start on your FIRE journey to start your own business. Too many entrepreneurs work their tails off to succeed *without* thinking this part through. You know what happens? Usually they don't succeed or even if they do, they're miserable. That's not the goal here. You want to *love* what you do while you make the kind of money you want.

The next four chapters (Chapters 4-7) are focused on what you need to know about your business before you even spend a dime on it. Oh, my gosh, if I had only had known these things when I was starting out! I would have saved so much time, energy and, yes, tons of money. I'm going to help you learn from my mistakes.

Chapters 8 through 10 are all about engagement marketing, using the power of the internet to build your business and to build relationships with your customers and clients. Some people cringe at the word marketing. But here's the deal: You can have the best service or most brilliant product the world has ever seen, but if people don't know about it, so what? Marketing is not optional. It's what will make or break you. The good news is that the engagement marketing process I'm going to teach you is incredibly effective and actually fun once you get into it.

So are you game? Even if you're not totally positive that this is for you, are you willing to give it a shot? I hope so because I'd love to see you doing what you love—and catching FIRE!

CHAPTER ONE

So, Whatcha, Whatcha, Whatcha Want?

One thing I've learned over the years is that, if you really want to start a business and be on FIRE, you need a strong motivation. You need to be absolutely, totally clear about *why* you want this. Let me just share what got me launched on this path.

It started on a Saturday afternoon. I was at breakfast with five of my girlfriends and all our kids. We had all gone to high school together and our children were growing up together. We were having a great time, laughing, reminiscing, with the kids all running around. It was like your perfect Saturday morning. My phone rang and, being a brand new real estate agent at the time, of course I answered it. A friend of mine from college was on the other end and she told me she had just seen my husband in Napa. I said, "Oh yes. He's there at a golf thing for work." She paused then said, "No Krista, I'm so sorry but, I saw him being intimate with another woman. Something's going on, Krista."

"One thing I've learned over the years is that, if you really want to start a business and be on FIRE, you need a strong motivation"

My heart started racing and I could feel my face flush. Tears instantly welled up in my eyes. I was hit with hurt and anger and an instant, crazy loop in my head: "But, we have kids. We built this life together. How many more lies did he tell? I just left my safe, full-time teaching job. How could he be so foolish to throw this all away?"

I remember driving home from the restaurant, doing my best to hold back the tears. Before I could even really wrap my mind around what was going on, I knew I was going to have to save myself. More importantly, I knew I was going to have to take care of my daughters and give them the life they deserved. I didn't know what that was going to look like. I didn't know how it was going to show up, but I remember a little voice saying, "Your world is about to change drastically, and you need to be ready for it."

In just a few moments, my world was gone, and I was at risk of losing everything. I panicked thinking I might lose my daughters, or they might not be able to live with me. I was freaked thinking my kids could lose their home, that they'd lose any semblance of normalcy being thrown back and forth between me and their dad. My life got so crazy. Within a week of my husband leaving me and tearing up what I thought was our happy home (I guess we all think that right before our world is torn apart!), I watched my two daughters being picked up from school by the new girlfriend who was driving *my* car! I mean who can even make up such craziness? Well, in a matter of days, this was my life. My why hit me like a ton of bricks: I needed to be able to support myself and my kids and give us a real life.

That vision and that why propelled me into becoming the rookie of the year in my first year in real estate. It got me to work smart and hard, selling 69 homes my first year and averaging at least one hundred homes every single year thereafter. My daughters and living in survival mode was the motivation that built my business and put me in the top 1% of all Realtors in the nation.

Why do I tell you this? Why am I telling you my devastating and quite frankly embarrassing story? Because I want you to see and realize that we are all the same. We are all made from the same thread. There is nothing special about me. I just made a conscious, consistent decision to move on, to fight and not let that devastating experience define me and the outcome of my new family, just my girls and me.

You just picked up this book and opened to this page. Why? What drew you to it? You may have just experienced a life crisis like I did. Your reason might be something really clear like, "I need to get the heck out of that crummy job!" or "I have a great idea for a business but no clue how to put it all together." Or you might just have a nagging feeling of wanting something more or different for your life. Maybe someone handed it to you and said, "Hey, you need to read this thing!"

I'm going to ask you to stop right now and ask yourself, "Why?" What is it that you're hoping to get from this book and why do you want this? Okay, maybe this seems like too much questioning right off the bat. But the thing I've learned is that no one ever gets anywhere if they don't have a vision. You can't get to Omaha if you don't have a vision of where Omaha is. You can't bake a great birthday cake if you don't have a vision of what that cake looks and tastes like. And you sure as heck can't create a great life for yourself if you don't know what that looks like either.

> "But the thing I've learned is that no one ever gets anywhere if they don't have a vision"

I also am a firm believer in the Universe, or God, or whatever you call your higher power. There is a reason you were drawn, referred or are reading this book. Your inner self is telling you that you may be meant for bigger and better things and that your mission in life has not yet been filled. My suggestion is that you just go with it and trust in the process.

In this book you are going to see TAKE ACTION sections

> These are things that you need to actually do. Stop when you see these sections. Take the time to work through them. If you're like me, you have a goal as far as how quickly you can finish a book. Well, I'm here to tell you that taking the time to work through the Take Action sections will be far more valuable than finishing the book quickly. To help you out, I've provided a workbook that you can download at TheBookFire.com Please download this now so you have it to work with. Even if an action exercise takes you a few days to work through, that's okay. In fact, that just means you're really taking this seriously and you want to see a true and lasting change in what you're doing. And quite frankly, it will affect the way your entire life plays out.

This book is all about how to turn your passions into a real live profitable business. The underlying reason any of us do this is because of something we want in our lives. Trust me, nobody works their tail off as an entrepreneur just for the heck of it! So if you're thinking of creating your own business, you need to figure out exactly what you really want. Otherwise, it's just not worth the effort!

You know what I always say to my coaching clients? "You have the responsibility to create the life you deserve." You can't just wait around for what gets handed to you. (Well, you can. But you probably won't get what you really want.) You need to create what you want. The first step is to get clear about your vision. If you've never even thought about what your vision is, I'm going to show you how to do that. For now, start with asking, "Why are you interested in *F.I.R.E.?"* Yes, stop right now and answer that question!

> " You have the responsibility to create the life you deserve "

Take Action #1

Take a few minutes and pull up the workbook. Write down why you were drawn to this book and what interested you. What do you hope to get out of it? Don't make this a big ordeal. Just write whatever comes to you. Then sit for a moment and think about it and write whatever else comes to you. This is meant to be fun and simple, so enjoy it!

Pick up the shovel -We're digging deep!

Now that you've answered that question (You have, haven't you? Don't cheat yourself, this is all about YOU and getting what you want out of your life.), I want you to go a little deeper to find your real motivation. For example, you might have said, "I want to make more money." Well, why do you want to make more money? "Because I want to be able to have a little more financial security." Well, why do you want to have more financial security? "Well, I want to make sure that, if anything happens to my husband, I'm okay." Now that's a pretty strong why.

It's not just that you want to make more money. It's that you want to make more money because you want to feel secure if something happens to your loved one. Or you want to make more money so when you retire, you can do it comfortably without the struggle. You want to be able to retire and do what you want to whenever you want to, without having to worry about whether you have enough money to support all the wonderful things you want to do. These wonderful things may include traveling, opening up a wine bar, visiting your kids throughout the country, being able to get weekly massages, playing golf whenever and wherever you want.

Or you want to make more money, so you can travel to all the places you're dying to see, send your kids to college, create a non-profit that helps

at-risk youth. It's really not that you want to add millions to your bank account. The money you say you want is for something that is important to you.

Or maybe you said you want to change your career. You really don't like what you're doing and you'd love to do something else. Maybe because you don't like what you're doing, it's causing you a lot of stress. And because it's causing you a lot of stress, you're fighting with your spouse. Because you're fighting with your spouse more, now you're depressed. And because you're depressed, your family is depressed. It goes way beyond the fact that you don't like your job. You're no longer a fun person to be around. You're not happy. It goes beyond, "Hey, I want to change jobs." You want to change jobs, because you want to improve your mental health and your life. You want to have a positive impact on people around you, not a negative one. You want to show your kids that they don't have to live like that, stuck in a job that makes them unhappy. That's your *real* why.

This sense of wanting to do something different is happening to so many people right now. It's so crazy. I'm in my 40's (you'll have to guess whether it's early or late 40's!) and it seems so many people my age are going through this. They are feeling like they just haven't lived up to their potential. They've been in a job where they have helped contribute to the wealth and success of someone else but haven't built their own wealth and success.

Or, they feel like there isn't any meaning or purpose in their profession. They know they could do more to impact and change the world. Some of them have a big, bright idea. They know if they could get that idea, product or practice out into the world, it would make all the difference— not only in their own lives, but to the lives of others. It could be their "Big Break."

My former employee, Sarah, started a bridal boutique. Her *why* was not just that she loved working with weddings and bridal stuff. She wanted to have more financial freedom, so she could be home with her kids more. She didn't want to have to work from 9:00 to 6:00 every day. She wanted to be free to pick her kids up from school and take them to school. Her why was, "I want to see my kids grow up. I want to be there for them, to be at their soccer games and volunteer in their classrooms. I don't want to continue to make my boss money, so my boss has freedom and time. I want freedom and time for myself!"

Working for me she realized that she could be her own boss. She could utilize all the marketing skills that she had learned from working for my company and apply them to her own business, and so she did. Of course, I was sad to see her go, but I also was thrilled that she had the courage to go out on her own. And trust me, it was a fabulous decision. She was making well over six figures within six months of venturing out on her own.

Okay, I can just hear some of you saying, "Nah. I don't need to do this exercise. When I set my mind on a goal, I do it no matter what. I don't need to waste my time thinking about my why. I'll just start my business." Really? How many wealthy and successful people do you know who are actually very unhappy despite all they've got? Maybe they went to law school and worked hard and built a great business—but they never really liked working in the legal area at all. Maybe they became a CPA because they knew they could make good money but now they are miserable because they have to work crazy hours during all the months of tax season. Maybe they started a retail business and make good money from it, but they hate dealing with all those grumpy customers. I can't tell you about how many stories I hear about attorneys who hate their jobs. So this step is important, and it shouldn't be overlooked.

"If you don't take the time to really figure out your motivation for starting a new business, you might end up succeeding—but you also might end up being miserable"

Here's my warning: If you don't take the time to really figure out your motivation for starting a new business, you might end up succeeding—but you also might end up being miserable. Digging into your why will prevent that from happening because you'll design everything around what you really want out of life.

Take Action #2

Take out the workbook and let's dig deeper. If you said you want to make more money, why do you want more money? What will you use it for? If you said you want to start your own business, why do you want to do that? How will that change your life? Whatever you wrote down in the first exercise, explore it more deeply.

Calibrating your GPS

After figuring out your why, you next want to ask, "Where am I in my life now? Am I happy with where I am in my life right now? Are there any things that I wish I could have done differently? Are there things that I wish I had done differently that I know I *still* can do differently?"

You don't have to drive yourself crazy with this. Keep it simple. Just write down categories in your life like career, relationships, fun activities, family, finances, health, maybe your personal or spiritual growth—basically any category that comes to you. Then rate how you feel about it from one to ten. One can mean "It's horrible!" Ten might mean "It's amazing!" and a five might just be "Meh."

Next, looking at those categories, think about what you wish you had done differently in that area of your life. Don't beat yourself up about it. Just notice some of the opportunities you didn't take or the not-so-great decisions you made. Maybe you took a job that got you nowhere or married someone who wasn't very supportive. Maybe you were too scared to try for medical school or you blew a chance to travel to Europe. Whatever it was, just jot it down.

Looking at those things—the things you did or didn't do that you wish you had or hadn't done—what would you still like to do? You can't go back and marry that guy who asked you twenty years ago. But you could still find a great life partner. You could still begin a different career or business. You could still travel. You could still get that tattoo removed or add one that has special meaning.

> "I believe that sorrow comes from the things we knew we should have started and never did. Even more so than the things we failed at but took the risk to try and learned something along the way."

I believe that sorrow comes from the things we knew we should have started and never did. Even more so than the things we failed at but took the risk to try and learned something along the way.

Take Action #3

Re-read the paragraphs above and answer the questions. Begin with the categories of your life and on a scale of 1 to 10, rank how happy or satisfied you are in each category. Next, paying special attention to the areas that have low rankings, what specifically would you like to change about them? Next think about some of the opportunities you missed or things you regret doing or not doing. We can't change your past but are some of your regrets things you could change or do in the present?

Creating Your Vision

Okay, so you have your baseline of where you are today. Now, if you could have your life look any way you want it to, how would it look? If you could have your dream job, live in your dream home wherever you wanted to be in the world, have all the things you want, and be with the people you really want to be with, what would your perfect life look like? Think about all areas of abundance, not just money. What would this perfect life look like spiritually, financially, your relationship with your spouse, your children, your friends and within the community? How would you view yourself and feel about yourself? What would it look like in your vocation, your job or career? How about your health, mentally, emotionally and physically? What could you be, do or have that would bring your level of satisfaction and happiness to a 10?

Remember, abundance is the whole spectrum of your world and the reality in which you live. When I talk about abundance throughout this book, please know I'm not just talking about money. I'm talking about your entire life both inside and out as a whole. The way you feel about yourself, your accomplishments and where you are in life are also a huge part of what I mean when speaking of abundance. As somebody or other once said, "Don't trade happiness for money." Sadly, too many people didn't listen to that wisdom.

What does your perfect life look like? Dream big here. Dreams can truly become our reality if we take actionable steps on a consistent basis to get there. That's what this book is meant to help you do. We are primarily focusing on the business aspect of it but remember where you see yourself and being able to attain that epic life, has a lot to do with when, where, and how you actually show up in your business.

TAKE ACTION #4

Using the questions above, sit down and journal about what all these areas would look like if they were all tens on the scale, your perfect vision. Check out the example below to get some ideas of how to put your vision together. I'd like you to take this seriously and really think about what you want. And don't get into thinking small: "Nah. That's never going to happen. I'll never get to have that or do that." I don't want you to shoot for just less miserable! If it's something you really, really want, write it down. You'll be surprised at how possible some of those impossible things can become.

This exercise may take you some time to do but it will be worth the time you put into it. And don't worry—it isn't set in stone! As you think of new things that would add to your happiness, you can add them and modify what you've written.

When journaling about your perfect vision, I'd suggest breaking it down in this manner: Daily, Weekly, Monthly, Yearly, Long Term. So you'll write about what a perfect day looks like and what a perfect week looks like, etcetera. Here is the example of my vision of how I want my life to look— and how I am actually living that life now.

Daily Vision: I wake up in the morning and spend the first 15 minutes deep breathing and thinking about how I want my day to unfold. I visualize myself being happy, having all things fall into place. *(Positive begets positive. You get what you expect, so start your day with positive thoughts)*. I go to the gym and exercise my body as I know this also exercises my mind. I come home and drink a healthy shake or eat a "clean" (sugar free, gluten free) breakfast.

I have the time and energy to make my husband the breakfast he needs to start his day off right. Of course hugging him and wishing him a great day is always a part of my morning routine. *(I don't take my marriage lightly, and I once read that hugging your spouse helps maintain connection.)*

I look at my day and prioritize the one major goal I'd like to get done and six objectives that will help me feel successful at the end of the day if I have met these objectives. (This is really important! When starting a new business, you're going to get through the week and often will feel like you've gotten nothing done! You'll get pulled in so many directions. But setting specific goals and objectives each day helps you see the mini wins throughout the week. You can look back and see that you've have accomplished more than you thought.)

I meet with my team to set goals for the week, make sure we are all on task, and help them focus to achieve their objectives. I schedule and block out time for my coaching business (commenting on participants' posts, giving feedback, coaching calls, and creating videos and trainings) and my own ongoing education to ensure we stay relevant and on the cutting edge of marketing ideas.

I end my work day by 5:00 so I have time to make a healthy dinner for my family. [This is very important to me. I had to create balance while creating my own new business. I found myself working 15 hours a day because I was so excited and couldn't stop. That's fine for a while and maybe a day or two a week.

But it's not healthy and can cause burnout. So get your priorities straight early on. Many entrepreneurs end up leaving a 9 to 5 job to work 16 hours a day, so be careful!) *In the evenings, I do something I enjoy, like spending time with my husband, children and jumping on the boat to putter around the Delta.*

I end my day at a decent hour by reading or listening to an audio book. I look at my calendar for the next day. I prioritize as well as visualize what I want that day to be. I give myself permission to dream about everything I need answered and for the correct "way" for it to show up. With as much positivity and gratitude as I can, I also think about all of the wonderful things in my life and experience in my day and all of the wonderful people and circumstances in it. *(Gratitude is one of the biggest attractors of abundance. Focus on what you are grateful for and you will receive more of it). The last things you think about are what you'll dream about and put forth while sleeping. Again, you get what you think about, even when you're sleeping. So, think and focus on good things so you'll manifest good things while you sleep.*

> "Gratitude is one of the biggest attractors of abundance. Focus on what you are grateful for and you will receive more of it"

I won't go through my entire weekly vision. But here's how it starts:

Weekly Vision: My work week is four days long. I work Monday through Thursday then take off Friday through Sunday. I make my work days into power days and get as much done as possible, so I can work only four days per week. *(I'm still working on this! I love what I do so much that I typically work six, not because I have to, but I LOVE what I do.)*

In your weekly goal, state how many days you'll work, and whether you'll work weekends or nights. If you don't want to work weekends and nights, state that. I want my weekends to be spent with friends and family, eating out at nice dinners or cooking a healthy meal at home. I also want to entertain on the weekends or take mini weekend trips either as a couple, family or with our friends. Write down your own vision of this.

When working on your monthly vision, start to project where you want to be in your business and your life. If you envision yourself setting goals and objectives each day and week, how will everything look in a month? Where would you like your business to be? What new things will you be doing or learning? How are things in your personal life with your family and friends?

Next tackle your six-month, one year and long term (three, five and ten year) visions. What does your life look like? What have you accomplished? What is different? What is better? How do you feel about yourself? What is new in your life? What have you discarded? (This is important. Many times we need to get *rid* of certain things, habits or even people in our lives in order to be successful and happy.)

Again, you want to take time to do this because your vision of the life you really want will help you figure out your specific goals. And those goals will tell you what action steps you need to take. For example, you may say something like, "By December 30, 20XX, I have created a course, created the means to properly market the course, and I have clients who have paid for the course and are now taking it." This is very broad and there are a lot of steps between here and there. But by starting with the end in mind and a date by which you want it, you can start figuring out the steps you need to take.

Also, as you start getting clearer on the type of business you want, it's important to make sure that the business fits into your vision. For example, if part of your vision is to travel the world but the business you're thinking of creating means showing up at the office every day, you'll need to tweak your business model.

Evolving that Vision

As I said, your vision and your why aren't written in stone forever. We change, and our circumstances change and what's important to us changes. You don't always have the luxury of sitting down with your journal to uncover your why. Sometimes, it comes flying at you like a tsunami. My own story from when I started in real estate is a perfect example.

Of course, not all whys come from disaster. Sometimes you can be motivated to change even if your life is really great. This happened to me just a few years ago.

One day I looked at my life and realized something was missing. This may seem crazy to you. I was fortunate enough to be extremely happily re-married. I had married Steve, an incredibly loving, loyal man who accepts me and all my flaws (trust me, there are plenty of those!). He was (and is) not only an amazing life partner but also a great father to our children. My children all turned out well (none of them are on drugs, living on the streets, or working as a stripper in Vegas). They're all amazing kids with three totally different personalities and career/college paths. Monetarily I was set, owning multiple homes outright and being debt free. I know people looked at me and thought I had it all. Sooo, you'd think I would be super extremely fulfilled, right?

Well, my friends, this is where the next why comes in. This may resonate with you and if it does, I hope you'll pay attention. I could have just stayed where I was in life, continuing in my very successful real estate career or I could dive back into my true passion, helping others and contributing to the world. The teacher was deep inside of me and had never left. As great as everything else was in my life, that gap left a place in my heart that was unfulfilled.

My prior why was to take care of my girls, and I had done that, including finding an amazing supportive partner who acted in the place of their absentee father. But, the real estate business felt so cutthroat. I felt as though I couldn't really share my talents and knowledge with my competitors because it would negatively affect my business. My love for teaching was not being met. I had mastered the real estate industry and I was ready for a new challenge. I wanted to help others achieve the success I had. I felt the need to make a positive impact on the world, to leave this earth better than when I entered it. When I'm helping others is when I feel the most alive and inspired myself. I was also tired of being tied to my phone.

So the why behind my new career of coaching, training and writing books has nothing to do with survival. Yet it feels as strong to me as when I was working to keep food on the table for my girls. When I hear about my coaching clients' progress and success, I find myself tearing up with happy tears. It's like I'm finally doing what I was put on the earth to do. To Serve!! It makes me want to leap out of bed in the morning (and I am NOT a morning person) and do all I can think of to do to encourage them. And that's how strong your why needs to feel.

When you tap into your real why, when you truly know what is most important to you, you'll push through anything and everything to get there. Trust me, to achieve your vision, you are going to go through more hard times than you think. It takes time and work. You need to keep your why and your vision in front of you so that when you feel like jumping off that bridge or diving under that rock, when you just don't see the light at the end of the tunnel and your head is way below water and you can't seem to catch your breath, you just keep going. With a strong enough why and a clear enough vision, you'll be able to see through all the obstacles to come.

> "When you tap into your real why, when you truly know what is most important to you, you'll push through anything and everything to get there"

Yes, You're Worth It!

One last question: Do you deserve to have your vision? That might sound like a dumb question but too many people are stuck where they are because they really don't think they deserve much more. They think the wonderful life they'd love to have is only available to people who are smarter, prettier, more talented, more educated, more experienced—more everything! Let me just say "Bull Shit!" (Sorry for cussing but in this case, it is super appropriate.) You are worthy! You are deserving! Love yourself for all of your brilliance and your weaknesses.

I see this often with women who have been stay at home moms whose children have entered school (leaving them with 8:00 to 3:00 to do whatever), or women who are empty nesters. These women spent their entire lives taking care of everyone else. Many women have been so engrossed with raising their families, they've put their own dreams, desires— and quite frankly their own identity—on the back burner. This is also true for women who are divorcees who find themselves alone after being married for some time (I know this because this was me). They relied on their husbands to be the primary provider and now find themselves starting all over with no idea what to do.

Many of these women end up working minimum wage or in dead-end jobs. It's so sad! These women (YOU) are smart and educated, yet they feel "less than" because they've been out of the workforce for so long. If this describes you, I am encouraging you NOT to settle. Don't just go take that job at Walmart or Target because you feel lost and worthless. You are NOT worthless, you can and are truly able and capable of achieving what you desire. But you have to believe you can. You have to believe in yourself!

You may have forgotten how great you are and how to tap into that greatness. In fact, hell, I'm going to just say that I think you're better off at this point. I mean how many men can handle taking care of a household for a weekend let alone for eighteen to twenty years while raising kids? So, put your big girl pants on! Say you can, say you will, say you are, and let's start DOING!

Many men are in a similar boat. They've stuck with a job that was the "right" job at one time. They've outgrown it now but worry that it's too late to make a change. Maybe they'd feel like an idiot, stumbling around trying something totally different than they've always done. What if the next job or business doesn't work out? They stay stuck where they are because they're just not sure they have what it takes to get what they really want.

There is so much potential and possibility out there in the world and it's up for grabs, it's up for the taking. The only question is, are YOU going to take it? I say, yes, let's do this!!

"There is so much potential and possibility out there in the world and it's up for grabs, it's up for the taking. The only question is, are YOU going to take it?"

CHAPTER TWO

Defining Passion

I'm guessing that you've heard that you need to "find your passion." I'll give you some exercises to help you find your passion in this chapter. But I'm warning you: Sometimes life happens and your passion actually finds you, like a gal I know, Natalie.

Natalie, had a pretty embarrassing challenge. After giving birth to her kids, she had that thing where you pee your pants. Any time she'd cough, she'd pee her pants. When she'd laugh or jog or jump, she'd pee her pants. Her worst day was when her aerobics studio was doing a live video demonstration. And right in the middle of it, on national TV, Natalie peed her pants! At that point, she said, "Oh, my god, I've got to fix this!"

> "Sometimes life happens and your passion actually finds you"

She researched it and found all kinds of information on nutrition and specific exercises that would help. Apparently, there's a whole science to it. Within a few months, Natalie had figured out what she needed to do and no longer had her pants peeing problem.

One day when she was working out, a friend of hers said, "Oh, man! I just peed my pants!" Natalie told her friend what she had done to solve the problem. Her friend said, "No, my doctor says this is common and that it always has to be this way." Natalie said, "No, it doesn't." The friend said, "You think you know more than my doctor?" The friend was almost arguing with Natalie that she was going to be stuck with peeing her pants forever!

Natalie got frustrated and went home and wrote a little mini e-book on how to not pee your pants. She made, I'm not kidding you, over $2 million in one year from this little e-book. She charged $27 for a book on how to stop from peeing your pants after you have kids and made insane amounts of money. And she has been able to help over 80% of the women who bought the book and had this problem. Helping these women became Natalie's passion.

Living Your Passion

What does "your passion" really mean? When you are doing something you're passionate about, you feel fulfilled and energized. You're so excited about what you're doing that it's hard to even sleep! You're so inspired, you can't put it down! You have to force yourself to go to sleep, or remember to eat, or to yank yourself off the computer and do something else besides pursuing your passion. (Be careful here. If you're like me, you'll be so engrossed in your passion, you'll forget to do all the things you need to do to stay healthy, like cooking homemade meals and getting enough sleep.)

Your passion is different than your vision though they go hand in hand. In your vision, maybe you spend loads of time reading because your passion is books. Part of your vision might be that you travel a lot because your passion is studying other cultures. Your passion is something that makes you feel fulfilled and joyful, so why wouldn't that be part of your vision?

The people who are most successful in this world have all based their career or business on what they're passionate about. I think many people feel like, "Oh, that can't be me. That's just for those guys who are really smart/talented/skilled. I haven't got a chance." Now, that might be true with winning the lottery. It's really, really difficult to win the lottery, like one in a bazillion. But it's not that difficult to create a business that can be fun, fulfilling, profitable, *and* is based on something you really, really enjoy. I'll show you how starting in the next chapter. You can do it, even if you feel scared to death or think that it is beyond your reach.

> "The people who are most successful in this world have all based their career or business on what they're passionate about"

What you are passionate about doesn't have to be some huge earth-shattering thing. Sure, you can be passionate about world peace or saving the planet. But you also might be passionate about quilting or collecting buttons or fixing old cars. You might get really jazzed about putting on parties or fishing or restoring antiques. Most people have several things they're really passionate about. For me, my passion is people. I love people and I love helping them. It's my thing. I can't describe it or why, but I'm in my zone when I know I'm doing good for someone else. When it comes to figuring out your passions and which passions you can monetize and create a business around, you want to begin by listing *all* of them. No censoring.

You don't want to confuse passion with something you're just good at. You might be a dynamite accountant or an amazing cook. But if you really hate numbers or cooking bores you, that's not your passion. You might be a really good listener but if you dread picking up the phone when friends call to whine about their problems, being a good listener is not your passion. A friend of mine happens to be good at a whole bunch of things from spreadsheets to running meetings to organizing events. It took her years to figure out that, just because you're good at something, doesn't mean you have to do it!

But if you do enjoy something you're good at, that can be golden! You just want to find a skill that is different and unique. It's especially great if you can find a broad skill then make it more specific and really detailed, to make it into something that could be really, really cool. Remember that just because something comes easily to you doesn't mean it is less valuable. Keep in mind that other people don't know how to do what you know how to do or can't do what you can do. They haven't figured it out. It seems simple to you, but other people still need help with it.

What if you have a strong interest in something, but you don't know enough to teach it or share it? Well, why can't you go out and learn? A teacher is somebody who just knows a little bit more than the person they're teaching. You need to target the people that you're two steps ahead of. You don't necessarily have to be the absolute expert at whatever it is.

Pondering Passion

Some people seem to be born knowing what they're passionate about. It's like they pop out of the womb and say, "Hey! I'm going to be a doctor!" or "I'm going to be a famous actor!" Your passion can be something you've loved since you were a little kid like camping or playing an instrument or making up games. As a kid, one of my mentors loved potato guns and he wanted to make one. He didn't know how so he just researched it and fooled around with it until he had made a great potato gun. When other kids saw it, they asked him all these questions. So he took every aspect of how to make a potato gun and created a little video training on it. He sold it online and made thousands and thousands of dollars — with just a potato gun!

A lot of us discover our passions through our life experiences. A friend of mine, Heather, kind of stumbled into her passion. She was in corporate real estate and traveled almost every week for business, flying across the country. On every trip, she'd buy a book to read on the plane, usually humorous chic lit. And she kept thinking, "Heck, I can write better than that." But she was working 60+ hours a week in a very stressful job and never had time to write.

Then one day, her back went out. She was laid up in fetal position for weeks and completely bored. So she laid in bed thought up a story for a book, making up characters and dialogue and everything. When she could sit up again, she typed it all up then researched how to get a publisher. Within a few weeks, she got a publishing deal for three novels! She left her job and started writing full time.

Another example is my former employee, Sarah. She was my marketer. I put her through a bunch of webinars and classes and she learned how to become an amazing marketer. At a certain point, she came to me and said, "You know, Krista, I want to go out on my own. I love you, I've learned so much from you, but I want to go out my own." I said, "No problem."

Sarah's passion and business idea came from when she got married. She had an amazing time planning her wedding. She loved hunting around for all the coolest doo-dads and making sure she got the best prices on everything. When her own wedding was over, she realized that there's money in weddings. Brides all want their day to be super special and they want to spend every dime they can to make sure it is. So, Sarah opened up her own little boutique. Now she averages anywhere from $12,000 to $20,000 a month on her boutique that sells all kinds of cool bridal stuff. She found that passion because she enjoyed putting together her own wedding so much.

A lot of people I coach found their passion through some kind of challenge they had or problem they had to solve like Natalie and her peeing her pants problem. Another example is a client of mine, Tiffany, who has a daughter with dyslexia. When her daughter was old enough to go to school, Tiffany had to really fight to make sure her daughter got the care she needed within the school system. She ran into the attitude of "Hey, your kid doesn't have a problem. Figure it out on your own."

> "A lot of people I coach found their passion through some kind of challenge they had or problem they had to solve"

So, Tiffany worked to understand the school system and how to get her daughter what she needed. She got really good at beating the bureaucracy. She even went so far as to go up to the state level where she got legislation passed that basically says dyslexia is a learning disability and schools are required to help children who have it. Other parents of dyslexic kids started asking her to help them. She became an advocate for children, helping the parents navigate the school system to get the help they really need. And she loves it!

Tiffany found her passion through solving her daughter's problem with the school system. Now, she helps parents out for free. She gets an incredible amount of fulfillment out of it, a "pay-it-forward" -type of thing.

My friend Raquel found her passion through a combination of something she loved and a real challenge. The thing she really loves is yoga. Her idea of the ultimate vacation was going to find a cool yoga studio or going to a yoga retreat for the weekend.

Raquel and her family are really active. They love the outdoors. They love hiking and camping. Every year, they went to Trinity to pick out their Christmas tree. But one year, Raquel got seriously hurt in an ATV accident. She severely injured her neck and started having constant debilitating pain. She could no longer do the activities that her family loved. She couldn't even go on their annual excursion to get the Christmas tree because her body couldn't handle the drive—and she's only forty six years old!

Raquel realized that her persistent pain was holding her back from enjoying her life and spending time with her family. She finally said to herself, "I need to get this under control." Raquel started flying around the state and going to different yoga studios. She got certified in every method of yoga you can think of. She learned techniques like the Melt Method from all these experts across the country. She just got really, really good at it, to the point where, finally, she realized, "Wow, I can do this!" She got certified to be a trainer and taught part-time at the gym.

When Raquel had gotten her own pain under control, she realized that she could help other people get their chronic pain under control, too. She had learned more than just yoga. She had learned that painful emotional memories can cause physical pain. So she learned techniques to work with that and developed her own techniques and methods as well. She started to notice that her biggest satisfaction came from helping people with chronic pain and that she was really good at it.

Based on that passion, Raquel created a new career for herself. She now works one-on-one with people who have chronic pain, especially people like pilots whose jobs often make the pain worse. Many of her clients have lived with chronic pain for years, and never thinking they'd be able to get better. Because of Raquel's own experience, she's able to help them.

A friend of mine told me another story about her veterinarian, Dr. Signe Beebe, who practices Traditional Chinese Medicine (TCM), using acupuncture and Chinese herbs with the animals she treats. She had originally been trained in regular Western veterinary medicine. But years ago, she had her own health crisis. She went to a bunch of doctors but none of them could help her, so she got worse and worse. Desperate, she finally went to a traditional Chinese medicine doctor who treated her with acupuncture and herbs. Within a few months, she was healthy again and she credits that doctor and TCM with saving her life.

So she started studying TCM and using it with her animal patients. She started seeing amazing results, even with animals other veterinarians had given up on. She kept studying Chinese medicine and using it in her practice and now teaches TCM to veterinarians all over the world—all because of her own health crisis.

Pursuing Your Passions

You probably figured out some of your passions just based on the examples I gave you. You may even already have a great business idea in mind. I'm still going to ask you to do the exercises in this chapter. Why? It will not only help you uncover more of your passions that could become businesses, but it will also show you themes and similarities in times that felt great to you. It can also add different dimensions to any business you begin. For example, maybe you love working on cars and you also love to write and draw. Well, you could combine those passions into an illustrated book about car repair, right? So pull out your journal and take a few minutes to answer the questions below.

TAKE ACTION #5

Finding Your Own Passion: Go back in your life and think about the times in your life when you felt like you were happiest. What were you doing back then where you felt like you had the most fulfillment, the most satisfaction, the most joy? It doesn't have to be something about work or your career. Maybe it was when you were getting married, or you were in college, or preparing for college. Maybe it was when you were becoming a new mom, or when you just started a new career. Stop and identify times in your life where you felt the most successful and happiest internally and jot those times down.

When you've identified times in your life when you were really happy, and felt fulfilled and successful, dig deeper and identify *why* that time felt so good. "What was it about that situation or about that period in my life that I enjoyed? What was I doing? How did I show up every day?"

A big portion of creating the success you want is defining your passion to make sure that, whatever you decide to do, you love it while you're doing it. It's super important. If you can identify a key period, or several key points in your life, when you were happiest, it will help you figure out what to do in the future.

Alex Charfen, one of my high level business coaches, has a class I went to called Momentum. He worked people through this exercise to really help them identify those fulfilling points in their lives and what they were doing when they felt at their peak state, optimizing at their fullest potential. He calls it "being in the state of momentum." It's okay to include those super joyful times like when you got married or fell in love, but I want you to dig a little bit deeper when you're going through this.

I knew I was ready for a change and I did this same exercise. When I looked back in my life, I realized that I really needed to be teaching again. Those were the times in my life that I was the happiest. Of course, some of the most amazing times in my life were becoming a mom, finding the love of my life and falling in love then becoming a wife. When I did this exercise a while back, I wrote down all of those things.

I realized, "Hey, one of the most amazing times in my life when I felt the happiest was when I was a teacher." First of all, it was an incredible journey for me to become a teacher. It took me five attempts and over a year to pass my test to become a teacher. It was agonizing and grueling! Then when I became a teacher, I was really, really good at it. The kids completely resonated with me, and I just loved reaching them and seeing their outcomes. I felt awesome seeing how different they were from when they started in my class to when they left. I remember having students who were miserably struggling, or who had gone to four or five different schools and been kicked out. When they came to my class, they just excelled!

I was really good at being a teacher and was just so happy while I was teaching. I had a ton of energy, and felt inspired to look for new, innovative ways to reach these kids, to make a difference and to make an impact. It was one of the happiest times in my life.

So, that was one of the times that I wrote down. Another time I wrote down was when I met my second husband and fell in love. Part of what was special about that time is that, for the first time, I felt safe and protected. I felt that I had finally found someone who loved and accepted me for who I am (and trust me that is an accomplishment all in itself). I could be myself and I didn't have to change. We had a lot in common and we did fun things together. It was just such a great, amazing time.

Of course, having my kids, and being a mom, and learning those experiences. That was, obviously, one of the most amazing time periods in my life. I felt a love I'd never felt before and was thrilled to have a part in helping them grow up as healthy adults. And it was so fun to cook with them and dance with them and watch them grow!

I remember how accomplished I felt when I graduated from college. I know this seems menial to many people, but I struggled with an extreme learning disability. I had worked my way through group homes and foster homes, so to graduate with a Master's Degree in Curriculum and Instruction made me incredibly happy and proud. At this point in my life, I realized that I love learning and excelling. I had to work harder than most to succeed and graduate because it did NOT come naturally to me.

> " My mantra was "Learn, implement, master, repeat "

I also realized that I really felt happy when I became a real estate agent. I very quickly rose to the top and I just excelled at what I was doing. It connected back to education and learning. I constantly educated myself, learned, and tried to improve. I'd study new tactics then figure out how to make them better. My mantra was "Learn, implement, master, repeat." I say it all the time to my students now. Learn, implement, master, and repeat. The thing about repeating is that, by the time you finally master something, you have to go back and learn about it again because innovations and better ways of doing things are always showing up. I did well in real estate because I constantly learned and educated myself to become better and stronger and this gave me a lot of satisfaction.

In writing these times down and digging into them to see what made them fulfilling for me, I noticed it always went back to the education aspect of what I was doing, the teaching and the training. I also noticed a theme of impacting people in a positive way. Whether it was working with my students or helping people make really good real estate decisions, a lot of my fulfillment came from knowing that my efforts had contributed to their happiness and success. I realized, "Hey, this is what I'm good at! This is what I love." That exercise helped me see, "I want to become more than a great real estate agent. I want to become a real estate coach." Then I realized, "Wow, I don't just want to teach agents. I want to really impact the world. I want to help and encourage people, especially women, so they know that there is so much more that they can do than just what they're doing!"

So, the first step is to look at what you loved and really enjoyed. Next, you need to ask, "What about that felt so good?" You will probably start to notice themes like I did. I noticed that I get the most out of my life when I'm helping other people and making other people smile. Seeing their growth gives me satisfaction, and I just love it! I love people! With people, you either love people, or you don't. I love, and enjoy people. I'm the kind of person who goes to a party and talks to everybody. I want to know all about them. I ask tons of questions and I'm very curious about them.

With this next exercise, we'll look at your passions from a different angle:

> TAKE ACTION #6
>
> Sit down, pull out your workbook and write down a list of things you're really good at and a list of problems or challenges you've overcome. Maybe you're really awesome at cooking, or exercising, or poetry. Maybe you're a terrific bargain hunter or you know how to keep your desk super-organized. Try to think outside the box a little bit. Next, think about problems you've dealt with as well and unique solutions you've discovered. Maybe you've figured out a certain way to garden that keeps weeding to a minimum. Maybe you've gone through a horrible marriage or a tragedy in your marriage, and you were able to

figure out how to get through it to have the marriage of your dreams. What skills did you employ? How were you different? What mindset did you use?

My husband's auto shop teacher always told him, "Find out what people really need, and what problem that they have that they can't really fix, then figure out how to fix it. Figure out how to fix the problem to make their life easier. Look for something that's not really out there yet, and you've got a huge, great invention."

Think about a problem you've had that you solved, things that you just enjoy doing in your everyday life, or ideas that you have that might enhance something that somebody's already doing. You don't have to be totally original. It can be somebody else's idea, but you have a different take on it or can teach it in a different way.

For example, I'm not the first person to write a book about turning your passion into a business. I'm not the first person to have these ideas I'm sharing with you. In fact, every idea that I have is just a spin-off from what people have talked about for hundreds of years. It's just the manner in which I internalize it, and it's the manner in which I express it, and it's who I resonate with. So, in other words, Tony Robbins might say something one way that won't resonate with you at all. But I might say that same thing using different words or examples and it will hit home for you.

> "You don't have to be totally original. It can be somebody else's idea, but you have a different take on it or can teach it in a different way"

Keep in mind that something that's easy for you isn't necessarily easy for other people. You may think that knowing how to pick up doggy poop efficiently is not big deal. But people have made a mint coming up with different types of pooper scoopers and poop pick-up services are in big demand! Maybe you helped your kids get through your divorce, and you and your ex figured out how to co-parent together without killing each other. Do you know how many couples are struggling with that? The tips and ideas you discovered so you could co-parent successfully could be a goldmine.

When you're first looking at your passions and your expertise, don't worry right now about whether it could be a business. Don't leave something that makes you happy or something you enjoy that you're good at off the list just because you can't see yet how it could become a business. Say you like making Halloween costumes for your kids, or you love to take karate lessons, or you really enjoy reading inspiring books. Don't worry about it. Just write it down and specifically what you enjoyed about the activity. Don't censor yourself right now.

It could even be something like you found this special trick when you're helping your kids' do their homework. You found a way to keep them engaged. Or maybe your child has ADHD, and you've figured out a certain way to get your child to eat healthy food. Maybe you've found a certain activity for your child to do that really cuts down their ADHD. Maybe you found it doing a lot of research or you discovered it on your own. That could be a little mini-course, or an e-book you can create because tons of people have ADHD (including me).

So take some time and think about all of this: things you love, the times you felt happiest, things you're good at, challenges you've faced and problems you've solved. In the next chapter, we'll get into how to turn those passions into a business you would love.

CHAPTER THREE

Can Passion Be Profitable?

Okay, so you have a list of things you love doing. Now what? The next step is to figure out all the ways you could turn that passion into a business. It may be totally obvious to you or it may be a total mystery. Either way, you'll do a lot of brainstorming in this chapter so you can come up with a business that inspires you!

And as I've said, even the simplest thing can become a huge business. Almost twenty years ago, a woman named Marla Cilley started a business that is now called FlyLady. It all happened because one day a friend of hers asked for help. Like a lot of women today, this friend was feeling completely overwhelmed between her work, her household, her kids, her husband and all the things she was supposed to keep up with. Can you relate? So Marla told her that the first thing she had to get control of was the "chaos and clutter" in her house because if she could feel on top of that, it would help her get on top of the rest of her life. Honestly, don't you feel better in a house that's clean and organized rather than one with piles of laundry, dead plants and a sink full of dirty dishes? Me, too.

So Marla helped her friend take baby steps (she has people start with just shining the sink every night!) in getting her house pulled together. And she helped her come up with a routine to keep on top of it. Then she got requests from other people and started helping other people do the same. She ended up writing a bunch of books and writing blogs. On her website, she sells everything from good cleaning tools to organizers and calendars. And it all started because she had become good at organizing her own household and wanted to help others do the same. So it doesn't matter how ordinary your passion is. You can still create a business out of it!

Let's look at a bunch of other examples:

A woman who loved animals lived in an apartment where she couldn't own any pets. She built a housesitting business where she stays in the homes (usually nicer than her own little place!) and gets to care for the owners pets. Another person I know doesn't stay in the home but goes in and feeds the pets, picks up mail and changes up lights and window shades so it looks like the owners are still home.

A woman who loves to bake, started a cupcake business. She not only bakes and sells cupcakes for special occasions, she'll also come to your house and put on fun "cupcake parties" where she teaches kids (or adults!) how to make cupcakes and decorate them.

A guy who loves to play golf put together a video series of "Best Golf Tips" from different teaching pros in his area. The pros get some exposure by being in the videos and he gets to have great information to sell online. He could even break it down further and have the pros give him "Best Golf Tips for Women" or "Best Golf Tips for Seniors." Golfers are always willing to pay to improve their game!

A lady who loves to salsa dance video-taped a bunch of step-by-step dance tutorials, everything from really basic steps to fancier routines. She also has blogs where she tells people where to find cool dance costumes and clothes—even the best underwear to wear!

I know of a number of people who are great organizers who have developed businesses around just getting organized. Some have created products: fancy bins, desk accessories, file systems, or daily organizers for specific groups like students, parents, even caregivers. Others have built "in your home" services where they come in and actually help you go through all the junk you can't quite figure out how to organize. Many of these services specialize in things like closets or garages or kitchens. Plus a zillion people have written books on organizing, right?

How many businesses have you seen around party or event planning? Some of us are great at this but many people aren't, so there's a big need out there. When my friend Colleen was in the corporate world, one of the things she loved was planning the company's events and conferences. Now she has her own business where she travels the world and handles logistics for all sorts of conferences.

What if you're an awesome teacher? You could start an online tutoring business using Skype. You could make a series of YouTube videos with creative ways to explain algebra or showing some fun projects for science fairs. You could write an eBook for parents about how to help children of different grade levels do their homework, or a book about how to keep your cool with your kids when doing homework with *(or for?)* them. I don't know about you, but many times I got more frustrated with the homework than my kids did.

Are you really good at running errands and dealing with vendors? You could start a concierge service where you pick up dry cleaning or shop for groceries or take elderly people to their doctors' appointments. You could get paid for sitting around all day waiting for the cable guy or staying with the plumber to make sure he does the job right. You could even do all the shopping for someone's Christmas list!

Let's say you have a love of prom dresses. This woman started a business where she took in used prom dresses and sold them or exchanged them for other used prom dresses. She bought some new dresses wholesale and created a boutique in a panel truck. She shows up with the truck so you can try on what she has. If you have a prom dress to recycle, you just pay the difference. If not, you can buy a dress outright. (I wonder if she'd recycle my first wedding dress!)

One young man who was pretty shy, did a lot of research on girls and relationships. With all this information, he started a blog and his first topic was "how to know if a girl wants you to kiss her." He now has a full blown business helping guys figure out how to approach a girl, how to get women to like you, how to get more confidence around women, etc. etc.

How about all of the issues around single parenting? Oh, my gosh! Anyone who has been a single parent knows that it's a crazy life with lots of challenges, especially in the beginning when you have no idea how to do it! Off the top, I can think of a million businesses you could create around that, everything from writing a book or blog to being a "parent for the day" to give single parents time off to setting up a help line for parents who just need to vent or get specific advice.

The Art of Doing What You Love

By now, you've got the idea, right? So let's start translating your passion into a potential business. I'm going to take you through a series of questions and I want you to really take the time to think about them. If you have a whole list of passions or skills, take just one of them at a time. By the time you finish this process, you'll know which ones you really want to go after.

To show you what I mean, I'm going to use the example of fly fishing. I know almost nothing about fly fishing so I'm going to make it all up and we'll see how it turns out!

1. **Who is interested in fly fishing?** Obviously, people who currently fly fish are interested and I'm just guessing the majority of these are men. I've also heard that there's a growing market of ladies who are interested in the sport. People who are outdoor types who are looking for a new hobby, maybe because they're retired now and have time on their hands, might be interested in fly fishing. So it could be anyone from a really experienced fly fisherman to a total newbie. Oh, and what about their families? They may not be interested in fly fishing themselves but they might be interested in finding gifts for their loved ones who fly fish.

2. **What do people who love fly fishing or want to do fly fishing really need?** Okay, so they need equipment. They need to know what the best equipment is and where to get it. And they need something to store it all

in and carry it all in. They need to know where to go fly fishing and maybe the best places in the world to go fly fishing. They need to know the rules of fly fishing or the etiquette (Is there such a thing?). They probably need to know something about fish, where they hang out and what attracts them. They need to know what clothes to wear (those crazy vest things and that funny hat) and where to get it. They need to know how to take care of their skin while fly fishing so the bugs of the environment don't bite them and the sun doesn't burn them. If they're beginners, they need to know all the basics of how to do it. If they are advanced fly fisherpersons, maybe they need to know how to enter contests to compete. Maybe fly fisherpersons need to know different exercises to build up fly fishing muscles.

3. **What are all the off-shoots of fly fishing?** I think there's a whole world of tying your own flies, like how to do it, where to buy the stuff you need, and knowing the best flies for different fish. How about handy food to take with you while you're fly fishing? Fly fisherpersons must need good places to stay and eat while they're on fly fishing trips. And what about the differences between fly fishing in cold weather versus fly fishing in hot weather? Does different weather require different equipment, technique or clothes? How about fly fishing injuries? Do they get some kind of carpal tunnel? And what about holiday gifts to give avid fly fisherpersons?

4. **What skills, talents, knowledge or experience can I contribute to the world of fly fishing?** Maybe you are really patient with beginners and a great teacher. Maybe you are the kind of person who researches the best deals or the best equipment. Maybe you are a great gadget inventor or you have a knack for drawing illustrations to explain things. Maybe you know a lot about exercise and how to get in shape for different activities.

5. **What other types of interests or activities would people interested in fly fishing like and where do they go?** (This will help you later on in your marketing endeavors, so it's important). So, they probably frequently go to outdoor and camping gear sites, right? I'm guessing they love being out in nature and probably interested in keeping the environment clean. As I understand it, the best fly fishing places are often very remote so maybe they are also interested in hiking.

6. **Based on this world of fly fishing, where do I want to fit in?** So maybe you're drawn to coaching women who are just beginning to fly fish. Maybe you could guide fly fishing trips that are both fun and educational just for women or seniors or kids. Or maybe you can think of some really cool gadgets you could create and sell that would help out in different fly fishing situations. Maybe you'd love to start a B&B near a great fly fishing area or start an online travel agency that specializes in the fly fishing excursions. Maybe you'd like to create videos on how to avoid injuries and stay safe while fly fishing. Maybe you can teach people how to tie their own flies so they don't have to purchase them.

The answers I brainstormed above are just a beginning (maybe I'd have more ideas if I had a clue about fly fishing!). When you're doing this with your own passion, you really want to spend some time and think of everything you can. Some of your thoughts may not seem to make a lot of sense but write them down anyway. When you're brainstorming, you need to stay loose and not critique yourself or your ideas.

If you get stuck, ask a friend to join you and brainstorm together. I don't know about you but I feel like when I'm helping someone else on their business, I know exactly who, what, when, where and how they should be running it, ideas and a blueprint comes to me so vividly. However, when I'm doing it for myself, I tend to get stuck. So asking for help may be invaluable to you. Along with coming up with ideas, friends often see talents and skills in you that you don't see.

> "When you're brainstorming, you need to stay loose and not critique yourself or your ideas"

Keep in mind that your business, just like your vision and passions, will change and grow over time. When I started my coaching and public speaking business, I started working with people in real estate because I had zillions of contacts and tons of credibility in that industry, I had mastered it, so it made sense to teach and help others. However, soon, I started coaching people in all kinds of fields because the basics of success are the same no matter what you want to do. And the marketing techniques of my business work whether you're selling fishing flies or coaching people on how to run and market their businesses.

Let's run the five questions through another example where the passion is healthy food. (HUGE market by the way!). BTW, if you're reading this and you live near me, I'd love to chat. I'm wanting to hire someone to help me cook/create healthier foods for the times I'm too busy to cook!

1. **Who might be interested in healthy food?** The first group I think of are moms who want healthy food for their families. People who have been given certain diagnosis or who have some kind of chronic illness, would be interested in healthier eating. Physicians and caregivers might be interested in healthy food plans or recipes they could give their patients. People trying to lose or gain weight, or who are determined to get into shape, would be interested. Women who are going through the change with hormones out of control and packing on pounds, would be interested in foods that can offset side effects of

menopause. People who are vegan or don't eat meat, or who are on a Paleo might be interested in creative ideas to change up what they eat.

2. **What do people who want to eat healthy food need?** They need to know that there is a difference between "dieting" and developing healthy lifestyle habits. They need to understand what a healthy diet looks like and maybe the specific foods they should eat based on their unique body type, objectives, or illness. They need to know how to cook things that are healthy and probably quick recipes that fit into busy lifestyles. They need to know things like the difference between healthy and unhealthy fats and the benefits of different herbs and spices. They need to know how to shop for healthy foods, how to read and decipher labels, and how to use ingredients they may not have used before. They need to plan their meals so they don't fall back into junk food when they're in a hurry. They need strategies on how to store the food and take it with them, or they need packaging products and storage. If they have kids, they may need to learn strategies to get their kids to eat food that is good for them. (They may need a strategy for their spouse as well!). They need guidance in how to order healthy food in a restaurant and tips to stick to their eating plan during the holidays. They need to know how to "cheat without really cheating" and how to make sweet or salty snacks that appeal to their appetite so that they can sustain their new healthy lifestyle.

3. **What are some off-shoots of healthy eating?** Sometimes people who want to eat healthy get into growing their own food and herbs so pesticide-free gardening is an off-shoot of healthy eating. People who want to eat healthy might want to eat out for a change and get everything from healthy pizza to a really healthy, fancy meal. What about organic wines? How about healthy eating dishware? (A woman started a business called Yum Yum Dishes -- that sells these cute little dishes to help kids with portion control.)

4. **What skills, talents, knowledge or experience can I contribute to the world of healthy eating?** Maybe you've been through a tough diagnosis yourself and learned about healthy eating through that. I am actually writing this book right now while on the beach in Hawaii (Don't judge me, I like to work and writing this book is more like a hobby and I LOVE it so it's not work to me, it's relaxing and I feel accomplished) and I met this woman who has Multiple Sclerosis and she is on a ketogenic diet. She told me that the inflammation of the disease has really diminished due to her new eating habits. This could be a new career for her. Maybe you've figured out clever ways to get your kids (and spouse!) to eat healthy. Maybe you're clever at planting gardens in tiny spaces and have created containers or have researched all the ways to get rid of pests without chemicals. Maybe you're good at making up fun children's teaching songs. Maybe you're just so darn enthusiastic about healthy eating that you inspire others. For example, my daughter had gained about 30 pounds in a matter of a year. It dramatically affected her self-esteem and self-

worth. I had tried to encourage her but it wasn't working. We ended up going to a healthy eating lifestyle coach. Our coach was so inspiring and encouraging and played a huge role in not only helping her lose the weight but also in boosting her self-esteem and self-image.

> "I LOVE it so it's not work to me, it's relaxing and I feel accomplished"

5. **What other types of interests or activities would people interested in healthy eating like and where do they go?** They may be interested in exercise and different ways to achieve their physical goals more quickly. They may be interested in other self-help types of activities, websites, forums, podcasts, magazines, etc. So they might hang out in gyms, go to self-improvement sites and blogs. They probably go to farmers' markets and sites that talk about the benefits of different foods. People interested in healthy foods are also often interested in information about alternative and natural healing.

6. **How do you want to fit into the world of healthy eating?** Maybe you feel called to teach moms how to prepare healthy meals. You could teach small classes or create an online video series or write a blog, eBook or book. Maybe you're into growing healthy foods. You could teach that or start your own garden or farm. Cool businesses have popped up lately where they deliver boxes of healthy ingredients (some of them all chopped up and ready to go) with recipes so you can put together a great meal without thinking about it. You could specialize in a particular diagnosis, say diabetes, and create meal plans and recipes that people with diabetes can follow. You could write a really fun children's book that encourages them to eat healthy and maybe start an online club where they get points and prizes for healthy eating. You could deliver healthy lunches to large business buildings to give people healthy choices for lunch. You could teach mindset trainings regarding food and healthy eating options on Facebook Live, YouTube, IGTV, Instagram, ebook, or podcasts.

Again, this is just the tip of the iceberg in terms of all you could do if your passion is healthy eating!

Profiting From Your Passion

Now it's time to run your own passions through the questions. Take them one at a time. When you've finished with one passion, tackle another. Stay loose and have fun with this! Remember that even the goofiest ideas can lead to something awesome. BTW, I recommend doing this on paper rather than on your computer if possible. Why? The physical act of writing apparently engages different parts of your brain and lets you be more creative.

"Remember that even the goofiest ideas can lead to something awesome"

TAKE ACTION #7

With one of your passions in mind, grab your journal and answer the first question. Write down as many ideas as you can before moving to the next question. When you have finished all the questions, take a highlighter and highlight the ideas that attract you.

1. Who would be interested in ___________________?
2. What do people who are interested in ________ need?
3. What are some of the off-shoots of ________________?
4. What skills, talents, knowledge or experience can I contribute to the world of ________________?
5. What other types of interests or activities would people interested _____________ like and where do they go??
6. Where would I like to fit in the world of ___________?

If you felt a little stuck doing this and you didn't come up with any good ideas yet, try going online and Google your passion (fly fishing, healthy eating, whatever.) You'll find more ideas than you know what to do with. Many ideas and businesses are started around people's passions. I typically don't have people do this internet search first because sometimes they get caught up in "But all the good ideas have been taken!" or "But everybody is already doing what I want to do!"

First, let me assure you that there are plenty of ideas that haven't been thought of yet and you can create plenty of variations on ideas—just check out how many different types of pooper scoopers there are out there! Also, the way you'll do whatever you do will be unique. People will relate to you who won't relate to the other guys who are doing something similar. On top of that, if there are lots of people offering a certain kind of product or service, it probably means that there is a ton of demand for it! Look to see what other people in your interest, business idea or passion are doing and see if it sparks some creative ideas of what you can do or a variation you can develop.

"Please understand that most of what people do or create is based upon an idea that someone else already was doing"

Please understand that most of what people do or create is based upon an idea that someone else already was doing. You can bet your bottom dollar I'm emulating other business coaches, digital marketers and public speakers because I want to size up my competition and ensure that I'm offering something that others may not.

You also might think about any seminars or trainings you've done related to your business idea. You had a reason for attending them, right? Whatever attracted you to that training will also probably be of interest to your potential customers and clients. Did you learn something at that seminar that you can incorporate into your new business? Try going to Amazon or audible.com and do a search on your passion. What books are available in your subject area? Do you see a spin off or variation you could apply to your new business idea? Don't let this Google search and business search throw you off. It is meant to spark some awesome new business ideas for you.

In the next chapter, we'll start fleshing out your ideas into a business model that fits the life you want to be living!

CHAPTER FOUR

Creating the Plan

To keep it simple, I'm going to distinguish between what I call a business model and a business plan. Your business model is like a basic overview of how you want your business to be. It's your vision for how you would like to operate. When we get into business plans, you'll get into the nitty gritty of your business like the resources you need and how you will find them along with what specific steps you need to take to put this together. How much is it going to cost to get started? What specifically will you do to market your business? That is all part of the business plan that we'll cover in the next chapters. In creating your business model, think about *what* you want it to look like and not yet *how* you're going to do it.

And just like your vision, start with the end in mind. Maybe you want to have a huge facility where you can teach auto mechanics to at-risk youth to give them a skill where they can earn good money. Great! Use that as your model. When we get into the business plan itself, you may see this model coming together in stages. You might start with teaching a few kids in your current shop in the evenings or find a parking lot where you can bring an old car and have kids come and work with you on it. Then you might build up to renting a space and getting equipment donated.

But in this section, envision the way you really want it to look when your business is successful and running on all cylinders! Keep the vision for your life that you put together in Chapter Two in front of you because your business model should fit in with that vision. Based upon that vision, think about the business model would give you that kind of life. It might not happen instantly, but what business model would help you get to the vision of your perfect life?

"keep in mind that, like everything in life, this model may change and evolve as you get into actually creating it"

As you're going through this chapter, unless you're totally clear about the business you wish to pursue, you may want to keep a couple of your business ideas from the last chapter in mind. And keep in mind that, like everything in life, this model may change and evolve as you get into actually creating it.

TAKE ACTION #8

This whole next section is your exercise! If you want, you can skim through it first then go back and actually answer all the questions. Or you can open up your workbook now and jot down your answers as you go along. Give each question some thought but don't stress over it. You can make changes when you review it all later.

How Do You Fit In?

Let's start by thinking about how you want to participate in your business. What kind of hours you want to work? Do you want to have to work nights and weekends, or do you want weekends and nights free? Are there going to be times when you don't want to be accessible to customers and clients? What are your time limits and boundaries? Do you want certain times that you can completely shut yourself down so you can enjoy your time off? Do you want your business to be part-time? Full time? Do you want your clients or customers to have access to you directly or indirectly? How involved do you want to be in your business, are you a silent partner or are you the main squeeze?

In your business model, do you see yourself supervising people, or always working on your own? What kind of work specifically do you want to do in your business and what do you want to farm out? Do you want a business that you can do anywhere at any time, or do you want to work out of a specific location?

Let's use me as an example. When I was on vacation with my family, I was up at 4:30 a.m. to do a coaching call with my clients then I was at the beach spending time with my family. I am able to take my business with me anywhere. If I only met with clients in person, I would not be able to do that. I realized this when I was developing my business model. I also knew that I was going to be traveling the country speaking, inspiring and encouraging others, but I still needed the one-on-one relationships with my students because this is when I'm most fulfilled. So I had to take that into consideration as I developed my business model.

Do you want to be "the face" of your business or stay behind the scenes? Do you want to deal directly with customers and clients or do you want to stay at arms' length and let someone else interact with them? If it's a product, do you want to manufacture it yourself? Do you want to oversee the manufacturing? Or do you want to hand off the whole manufacturing part to someone else?

Location, Location, Location

Do you want a bricks and mortar type of thing or do you want a business that can operate on the internet? Do you want a business that requires you to travel to customers and clients or do you want to interact using technology? If your business is some kind of coaching, training or educating service, how do you want to interact with clients and students? In person? Online? With evergreen webinars you create? Do you want a business where you have to be in a certain geographical location, like near a lake or in a climate where you can grow coconuts?

Does Size Martter?

Do you want to grow this into a family business? Do you see more than one product in the future, or a line of products? Or do you want to stick with just one thing? Do you want your business to be a local business, or do you see it going national, even international? Don't be afraid to go big here if that suits you. And don't feel that you have to be a huge business if you really don't want to. Success means different things to different people. So stay true to yourself, map it out in your mind, visualize the mental picture of the end result you want on a regular basis. Your mind will work to help you get there.

> " Don't be afraid to go big here if that suits you. And don't feel that you have to be a huge business if you really don't want to "

Do you eventually want to train people to teach what you teach? Do you want to expand your coaching or training to other types of clients or other subject matters?

Letting The Garden Tend Itself

If you are thinking about training or coaching services, one business model is the evergreen product model. An evergreen product is something like writing a book. You write a book once, you've written it. You're done. You can create a video or record a training call, then you're able to use it again, and again, and again. You do something once, and you can use it for the next batch of students, or the next coaching group. All of those are evergreen products.

You can create an evergreen product with just about anything. For example, in my mastermind group, we have people who are creating evergreen products around being great at barbecuing. They create videos one at a time on different topics on barbecuing then sell them. You only have to create the product once. However, you do have to constantly market that product! We will get into the marketing later on in the book. This is an essential piece of the pie and a large focus of this book.

Quality Counts

Another aspect of your business model is the level of quality you want in your business. Some people might want to make a little ragtag video and sell it for three bucks. Some business models and evergreen products are meant to be super, super affordable and easily obtainable so you can reach the masses. If you promote it well, anybody and everybody will buy it. You can make a lot of money that way.

Other people want to put their heart and soul into what they offer and deliver incredible value. Obviously, that comes at a higher price to produce and you'll need to charge more for it. Not everyone will be able to afford what you offer. People are definitely willing to pay more money for something they see value in. If they see immense value and know what you offer can change their lives, they're willing to pay just about any amount of money for it. But the value has to be there and your target market will be smaller than less expensive products. But trust me in this, if you offer enough value and your prospective client or customer can see it, they'll find the money. A buy decision is typically not about the money but about their perceived value of what you're offering. They will find the money if they know it can make a true difference in their life.

> "A buy decision is typically not about the money but about their perceived value of what you're offering"

There is no right or wrong. It's what you're comfortable with. Keep in mind though that higher priced, higher quality products usually require a higher level of involvement from you.

If you're aiming for high quality, it doesn't mean you need to stop and wait until it's perfect. Get something out there now, then always improve upon it. Change it, make it better. But ask yourself if you are going to be a McDonald's or a Ruth's Chris Steakhouse. Who are you trying to attract? Is it an information product, where there's nothing else involved, like ongoing customer service and support? Higher-end products offer a lot more support and involvement on the back end. If that's your business model, you need to think about how you'll provide that extra support. Will it be you, or will you need help?

Bull's Eye!

We're going to get into this in A LOT more detail in future chapters because figuring out your target market is critical to your success! But for now, who do you want your customers or clients to be? Are they a certain demographic, like teenage girls or people over sixty-five? Are they a certain nationality or do they have a certain occupation like teachers? Are they people with a certain issue or problem, like people who want to lose weight? Do they live in a certain area or can they be reached anywhere by any means? Make a note of the types of people you would really like to work with.

Money Motivation

When your business is fully operating, how much money do you want to make? Don't just say, "I want to make a bazillion dollars a year!" Don't just throw out a number like "$85,000." Really think about it, why you want that money and what it represents. Will this business be your sole source of income or will you continue to do other things that make money? Write down what you'd ultimately like to be making from your business. If your business is to be a non-profit, are you able to make money from it? Where will the funds come from to support the non-profit's mission?

Remember that money in and of itself is not a good enough motivation. The question is, "Why do you want to a lot of money? What's your end result?" Do you want to make a lot of money so that you can support your family and go on vacations without stressing and worrying about work? Do you want to make just enough money so you know that you're going to be able to retire comfortably without worrying? Dig a little deeper than just, "I want to make this amount of money." Focus on what making the amount of money will mean in your life.

Your Purpose

Of all the questions I've asked you, the number one thing you need to think about is your purpose. What's the purpose and mission for this business? What's the ultimate outcome you're after? How will it contribute to your life? How will it contribute to your community or the people who become clients or customers? The purpose of your business should be something you can get really excited about. When you think about your purpose and what your business will contribute, it should make you proud, like "Hey! I've taught people how to make the best darn fishing flies ever created!" or "My t-shirts will make people smile and feel better about the world and themselves." "I'm going to positively affect every life that I touch." What is your mission and purpose? Don't overlook this. It's important and will affect every aspect of how you set up your business model.

Do the Pieces Fit?

Now comes the first test: Take all of those things you've jotted down in your workbook and if you haven't done this yet, stop right now and do it. Next, look at all of your answers to the business model questions, and see if they make sense together. If not, something's got to give!

For example, say you're thinking that you want to open up a boutique and you don't want to supervise employees. If you're opening up a bricks and mortar boutique and you don't hire employees, you're probably going to have to work weekends and nights. If you don't want to work weekends and nights, but you still want to do boutique-y type things, maybe you need to consider an online boutique. You get a call service (that you wouldn't really have to supervise) to assist you with orders on the weekends and nights, or you can set it up so that people place orders online. Then you can either do the packaging and mailing during hours you want to work, or you can have a fulfillment house do it.

If you want to be a coach, like a business coach or health coach, typically you will work with people one on one or in groups. But say you don't want to travel and you want to do all of your coaching from your own home. With some coaching, you need to be physically present with the person. But with other types of coaching, you can work with people remotely via phone, Zoom or Skype. What about the hours you want to work? Are you going to allow clients to have access to you all the time, or is it only going to be during your coaching sessions? Will you do group coaching sessions? Do you want the group to be able to ask you questions during these sessions? Or are you the kind of person who gets thrown off, so you just want to do the presentation you've prepared without interruptions?

> "You've really got to properly set expectations and boundaries with yourself and with your prospective clients and customers"

I know it seems like a million things to think through, but I've learned a lot from my own business, things like, "Wow, I should've created more boundaries," or "I shouldn't have given people my personal cell phone number." I could have had clients use Voxer, which is like a walkie-talkie thing where they don't have my own personal number. If I had given more thought to what I really wanted my business to look like, I could have set clearer boundaries and expectations as far as, "Hey, it could be several days before I get back with you, because a lot of these questions can get answered on the group coaching call." You've really got to properly set expectations and boundaries with yourself and with your prospective clients and customers.

Whatever your business will be, sit down and visualize, "How is this going to work?" Really play it through asking, "Okay if this happens or that happens, how do I want to handle it?" You won't be able to anticipate everything. You don't know what you don't know, right? But ask yourself questions like, "How big do I really want to get? How many clients do I want to handle? How many products do I really want to sell?" "If I get hit with a ton of orders during the holidays, where will I keep all the inventory?" "What parts of my business can someone else do if I get crunched for time?"

If you want to combine a couple of things in your business, how will those play out? For example, say you want to be a public speaker and you want to coach people. With the speaking, you're going to be traveling a lot, but also need to keep up with the students you're coaching. Your clients may need to be flexible regarding schedule, so you can fit in your speaking gigs. You may need to make sure you always have good cell or internet connection wherever you are, so you can handle your coaching calls.

If you're thinking about products, think really carefully through how big you want to get. The size of your business makes a big difference in terms of how much inventory you need, and how much space you need in a store or storage facility. Will you have to rent space? Will you need people to track inventory and do packaging when you get to a certain size? Are you going to produce the products yourself? If not, will it get manufactured here or in some place like China? If that's the case, how are they going to fulfill it and actually get that product to the customer? Will you do it or someone else? This is all part of your business model.

Finding Your Niche

In his book, *Expert Secrets*, Russell Brunson talks about "finding your blue ocean." A "red ocean" is a market that has thousands of fish. But because so many sharks are already feeding on fish in that market, the water is blood-red. You've got to figure out your niche, your own sub-market, and what is unique about what you offer so that the water is blue and full of fish but not full of sharks.

This doesn't mean that just because a lot of people are doing what you want to do, you can't do it. It just means that you have to distinguish yourself and find the specific niche that hasn't been tapped into as much. How are you going to make your product unique, and better, and stand out? What specific need are you going to respond to and how are you unique in how you respond to it? What are you going to fix and how is your solution a little different than anyone else's? How can you tailor what you have to a more specific group, like not just women but women who are active seniors?

"What is the one way that you can tweak something or emphasize something, so you can really stand out?"

Think about it: If whatever it is that you're offering is generic and already out there, that need's already being met. You're not standing out within all the noise. You're just like everybody else. You've got to figure out, "What is the one way that you can tweak something or emphasize something, so you can really stand out?" Review the questions in Chapter Three to help you brainstorm and come up with ideas.

For example, in my real estate coaching, I can say, "Hey, there are tons of real estate agents and coaches out there. They teach many of the same things, but very, very, very rarely are they teaching how to use video, and how to repurpose video, and how to work with social media effectively, or how to target market and re-target, or how to use Fortune 500 digital marketing strategies to reach your market. It just doesn't get done." Another way that I stand out is that I'm actually a real estate agent who is in the Top 1% in the nation. Many coaches become coaches because they themselves could not sell. Have you ever heard of the saying, "If you cannot do, then teach?" Well, I am exactly the opposite. Not many other real estate coaches have personally achieved that level of success. And because I've built my own extremely successful business from scratch, I am unique among business coaches as well.

Early on in my coaching business I realized by allowing certain people to enter my program for free (Yes, for free! I have a strategy for doing this that I will discuss later), I realized that the techniques I teach work for ALL businesses. Why would I limit my trainings to just real estate agents and not share it with other budding entrepreneurs? So keep in mind, your business model will evolve.

Let's take another example: What if you want to teach sewing skills? There are a ton of sewing tutorials on-line, so what could make yours different? How about targeting men who want to learn to sew? Maybe you come up with sports analogies to help them understand what you're teaching. Maybe you focus on sewing projects that men would especially like to make, like sewing a fly-fishing vest! Or maybe you target people who want to sew fast and cheap. You can come up with different ways to sew super cool clothes or crafts using recycled clothing or old sheets. You could teach sewing short cuts and hacks or how to sew a dress in under an hour. You can come up with a zillion ways to become a specialist as a sewing teacher. But staying in the "red ocean" of generic sewing teachers won't get you very far.

Riches in Niches

A lot of times, people are afraid that, if they specialize in something, it's going to limit them. What you have to understand is that it's completely the opposite. The more that you specialize in something and the more that you're known for that one thing, the more that you're going to be sought after for that one thing. The rest of the world will still find you. But the people you really laser focus on, your niche, can't help but be attracted to you. You end up getting the best of both worlds.

> "The more that you specialize in something and the more that you're known for that one thing, the more that you're going to be sought after for that one thing"

When it comes to your specialty and your target market, it's like the chicken and the egg: Which comes first? Actually, it can be either. You can come at your niche and target market from either direction. You can start with your target market and figure out what they need, or you can start with something that you want to do and figure out who your target market would be for that thing.

For example, you can start with, "Over-stressed housewives are the people I want to work with." Then sit down and ask yourself, "What problems do they have that I want to solve for them?" Or, you can start with, "This is what I want to teach. I want to teach how to clean your car." In that case, you sit down and ask, "Okay, so who are the different people who would be attracted to that?"

The Profit Persona

I always have my clients create avatars, using either people they know or making up a character who perfectly fit the profile of their target market. It's easier to understand and become familiar with a specific individual than a whole group of people, right? For example, it's easier to think about what Auntie Thelma likes and needs versus what the whole population of elderly ladies want and need.

I like to have a couple of avatars, either real or made up, who have all the characteristics and traits of the people in the market I'm targeting. Start by asking the basics: What age range are they? What sex? What educational level or socio-economic level are they? What do they know or not know about what I have to offer? Are they single, married, in a family unit?

You want to ask, "What are their wants and desires?" People don't buy what they need, they buy what they want. What they want actually fills their needs, in most cases. You need to figure out, "What is it that these people want? What do they desire, what are their wants, and how will those desires really fulfill their need?"

You need to know everything about your avatar so that you can learn to attract that avatar and be where that avatar is. What kind of websites are they on? What kind of books do they read? What are their interests? All of those things make a difference in terms of where and how to market to them. It also makes a huge difference when you're thinking about how to design your product or service for them.

Again, who do you want to work with and who is most likely to buy from you? Let's really narrow this down. Let's just say you think you're going after moms. Is it a teenage mom, a young mom in her 20s? Is it a mom with kids who are just starting school or moms whose kids are going off to college? Is it a single mom, maybe who has recently gone through divorce? Is it a mom who had children older in life? Is a mom who is in the loving marriage?

You might be thinking right now, "Holy crap, Krista! How do I know?" But here's the deal: The more you identify your exact client avatar, the more you'll know how to reach them, what copy to use when writing to them, what language to use when speaking to them. You'll have a clearer idea of what they need, what did they want, what they like and what did they dislike. All of this is important. And here is the big kicker, ultimately by taking this seriously, it will save you time and money. Yes, re-read that: It will save you time and money. And to me, my time is even more important to me than money.

> "The more you identify your exact client avatar, the more you'll know how to reach them, what copy to use when writing to them, what language to use when speaking to them"

When identifying your avatar it helps to actually put pictures of them on your wall. Cut them out from magazines or get a photo of the real person you used to create your avatar. I have pictures of my avatars on my mirror so every time I brush my teeth, I'm looking right at them. I know this sounds nutty but the more you can immerse yourself and really get in your avatar's head, the easier your business will be, everything from marketing to designing what you're going to offer.

TAKE ACTION #9

Go to your workbook and create a few avatars right now. You can use a real person or make up a fictional person. Remember, your avatar is your perfect customer or client, the one who you really want to work with and the one who will be most attracted to what you have to offer. Get specific: What age range is this person? Where do they live? Occupation, education level? Married, single? What are their interests? How much do they know about what you offer? What are their problems and issues? What do they love? Answer these questions for at least three avatars.

Notice that your avatars may be slightly different from one another. One might be married with kids and another might be single. But the point is to start narrowing down who your avatars are and start understanding them, so you can offer what they really need and target them in the marketplace, so they know about you.

Your avatar also tells you who or what you want to associate your products or services with. For example, if I am targeting women who are going through menopause and experiencing hormone changes like hot flashes, weight gain and sleepless nights, (Sorry if I keep bringing this up! I'm in that group so it's on my mind!), what else may they be interested in? They may be interested in exercise websites, healthy eating websites, books, or podcasts. They may be looking at alternative healthy methods of controlling hot flashes or hormonal homicidal urges. You may be able to create an affiliate partnership with other businesses who will promote your product for a fee. Or, you may be able to study those websites to see what wants and desires are of your avatar they are featuring. Pay attention to the copy, headlines, and language they use. You not only want to mimic the good things you see but you also want to kick it up a notch to make it better and stand out.

Creating a good avatar is important. It will save time and money because you'll be marketing to the appropriate people, the people who are most likely to want what you have to offer. Spend some time researching them so you know how to give them what they need. You'll save time and money on your marketing by going after the right person in the right way with the right service or product.

It's not just as simple as creating a dynamite product because you still have to reach people. You still need to get people to see you and know about the product. Marketing will be a huge part of your business and can't just be an after-thought. I think part of what happened with me and a lot of other people is that they thought that they could create a great product and—boom!—instant success. Not gonna happen. We'll spend several chapters on marketing, so you don't make that mistake.

Your avatar may change over time. Who you think your avatar is now may not actually end up being the case. Your analytics and target marketing will help you assess your best target market, so you can change or modify this in the future.

Let's think about some example avatars. Remember the story about the woman who peed her pants and wrote the eBook? After that, she began a business called Modern Mom Lifestyle that offers all kinds of things like cookbooks for fast, healthy meals, tips on being organized, tutorials on doing your make-up in under five minutes. Her target market is, of course, busy moms, especially moms who work outside the home, most likely in white collar jobs. Their age ranges from 24 to mid-thirties. They are probably educated and research healthy alternatives in lifestyle and eating. She wants more time with her kids and she probably involves them in activities like sports, dance, school activities or community projects. She wants more organization. She wants more personal time. She wants her life back while still being an amazing mom. She might be a career person who wants to learn how to manage working and be great on the job while still being a great mom. She wants acknowledgement for her wins and successes outside of the home (because we all know that being a mom is a thankless job! No one appreciates all you're doing until ten years after the kids leave home!).

Another person I admire is Molly, who is in my master mind group. Molly started a business based on boudoir photography where she teaches other photographers how to do it and create a business out of it. People in her target market are mainly professional photographers who have been in the business for several years, so their age range is probably 35 and up. They are probably entrepreneurial, maybe more gutsy than some of their peers. Though they are artistic, they have a practical side. They need more clients and want to make more money doing what they love doing. They also may want to control their schedule and have more free time rather than working at weddings all weekend.

Francel, a client who has a business devoted to helping nurses live healthier, happier lives. They're typically women who are at least in their mid-40's who have been in the nursing industry for some time and are worn out. Obviously, they are educated and love helping others. Because they are in the medical profession, they are used to research and researching online. They have probably joined groups and associations for professional development and to keep up with the latest developments in medicine. These nurses still want to help people because that's why they got into the profession. But they're tired and stressed. Maybe they don't realize just how hard the profession was going to bethat they'd be spending a good part of their day cleaning up barf and bedpans. They've been so busy worrying and helping their patients, they've forgotten the importance of taking care of themselves and are too tired and exhausted to figure out and remember how to do it.

"You want to be able to describe your avatar as you would describe a close friend or family member"

Get the idea? You want to be able to describe your avatar as you would describe a close friend or family member. Think about their needs, what they like, what they hate, even imagining how they talk can help you when it comes to your marketing and designing what you have to offer them.

Branding

Your brand is built around your niche and your target market and is part of your business model. Don't wait to develop your brand. Just do it. One of the biggest mistakes you can make is to wait for everything to be perfect. I think a brand is important, but I think it should evolve. Not everyone's going to know you at first anyway. So just get out there and get comfortable marketing yourself and your business. Think of a good name, something that says what you do and reflects who you are if possible. But even if you can't come up with a brilliant name, don't let it stop you from just starting. Just do it, just start!!!

Too many people get some great big idea then let their fear take over. They get on these rants. They overeducate themselves. They take too many classes. They worry about the branding. They worry about the equipment. They worry about everything being so perfect and they don't get out there and just get started. Again, that was one of the biggest mistakes that I made.

"Too many people get some great big idea then let their fear take over"

Please people don't let your excuses about making everything just perfect be your excuse. Bottom line is it is just that, an excuse and another reason as to why you are not moving forward. Quit being a victim of your excuses. Just start. How do you eat an elephant? One bite at a time. How do you propel yourself forward? By starting. Just start! Think about when you plant an apple tree or a cherry tree. You don't see fruit right away, it's just a seed. Finally a sapling pops up and in a few years, you have more apples than you can give away. But if you never planted that first seed, you'd still be looking at dirt and buying your fruit from the store.

"Quit being a victim of your excuses"

Branding is important but it's not going to make or break you. Think about your business's name. Make sure no one else has a name that is very similar to the one you choose because it will make it harder for you to be found. Make sure that the name has something to do with the audience you're trying to reach and what you're trying to accomplish with them or the outcome. For example, Modern Mom Lifestyle is clearly directed at moms and their lifestyle. Seven Figure Real Estate Blueprint is clearly directed at people in real estate who want to make a lot of money.

When I first made my Facebook group page, I titled it Krista Mashore Coaching. That name basically stunk because it was about me, and not about the results I was offering to my target audience (my client avatar). I changed the name to 7 Figure Realtor Blueprint, and we grew to over 2,000 members in a matter of 3 months. People didn't give a hoot about Krista Mashore Coaching but they were very inspired to join a group that would give them a blueprint for making 7 figures!

The Business Model Conundrum

I've put together a couple of brief examples to help you get started on your business model. I'd like you to go into more depth when you do yours, but don't stress over it. You can always come back and change it later. But it's important to get something down on paper. (You'll see the set up for fleshing out your business model in your workbook under Take Action #8.)

Example #1: Bed and Breakfast Relief Person: This is a business idea where you go into different bed and breakfast inns when the owners go on vacation.

> **Your Participation**: My spouse and I will work two to three weeks per month and we will be available during major holidays. While we're on duty at a bed and breakfast, we will be available to do everything from the cooking to managing reservations (not maintenance or housework) depending on the size and need of that inn.
>
> **Geography and Location:** We will be available to go anywhere within the contiguous United States (not Hawaii or Alaska) because we will use our RV to get to each location.
>
> **Size and Reach**: Initially, it will just be my spouse and me. Eventually, we may add our two married children and their spouses if the business warrants it. But we don't wish to bring in relief teams other than family.

Evergreen Products: We might put together a manual for running different sizes of bed and breakfast inns down the road and sell it. We might also put together a training program for people who want to do what we do.

Quality: We have both completed accreditation courses and have worked in hospitality, so we offer a high quality of service to our clients. Plus, we are able to provide almost anything an inn requires, from accounting to cooking.

Your Target Market: Our clients will be higher end inns that have received great reviews from guests and have a reputation for excellence.

Money: Once we are fully up and running we will make $90,000 per year from our business. This will allow us to travel, have time to visit our grandchildren and add to our retirement fund for the next fifteen years.

Purpose: Our service will allow inn owners *real* time off, where they can relax and enjoy their vacations (or handle their family emergencies) knowing that their B and B is being cared for and managed to the same standards they have themselves. We also will make sure their guests have an excellent experience.

Example #2: Puppets: This is a business where you make and sell puppets.

Your Participation: I will work four days per week for ten hours each day (Wednesday through Saturday). I will design the puppets and create prototypes that I can train others to manufacture in their own home. I'll be the quality control, checking to make sure every puppet is perfect. My wife will handle accounting and my son will do the shipping. We will all take two weeks off during February for our annual family reunion.

Geography and Location: I will sell the puppets online, so customers can come from anywhere. My office and design center will be in my own home. My puppet makers will all be local, and inventory and supplies will be stored in my son's garage.

Size and Reach: I would like to produce around 60,000 puppets per year and reach people all around the world.

Evergreen Products: I would like to produce training videos for educators and parents that show how to use puppets to help children deal with difficult times like parents' divorce or illness.

Quality: Our puppets will be high-quality, all hand-made and meant to last for years and years. I will provide designs that are unique.

Your Target Market: My target market is teachers, schools, pediatric psychologists and psychiatrists as well as parents of children with mental/emotional problems.

Money: I would like to make an income of $100,000 per year so my wife and I can both leave our other jobs (that are becoming too difficult physically as we get older).

Purpose: We want our puppets and the training we can offer to help children deal with their emotions and problems. We want to provide an excellent tool for parents, counselors, and teachers. And we want our puppets to be so unique and beautiful that they are recognizable as coming from us!

Got the drift? Now go to your workbook and create the model for your own business idea.

CHAPTER FIVE

The Actual Business Plan

Why do you need a business plan? Okay, so here's a true confession (Don't judge me!): I didn't start my new business with a business plan or even a clear business model. But I realized early on that I needed one because I found myself trying to do everything at once and going off on tangents that didn't even matter. I wasted a ton of time and money because I hadn't taken the time to get totally clear on what I was after and the steps I needed to take and the order I needed to take them in. Oh, and let me just repeat myself, I wasted a LOT of money!!!!

> "A decent business plan will not only help keep you on track. It gives you direction when you run into obstacles"

A decent business plan will not only help keep you on track. It gives you direction when you run into obstacles. Here's the deal folks. In getting your new business off the ground, you'll probably have times that you feel like giving up, maybe even going back to your old, unsatisfying life, because it's comfortable. Whenever you feel gloomy like that, envisioning your business model and looking at your business plan helps you to keep moving in the right direction. And having a clear vision and purpose will give you the inspiration to keep you going.

The business plan I'm talking about here is not the big formal plan you might put together for an investor. This is for you and the people working with you. Keep it short. Bigger is not better in this case. Your plan is there to ensure you know where you're headed. And please understand that, just like anything in life, your business plan will change. When you start any kind of business, you seriously have no idea about what you have no idea about. You'll find out that you don't know what you don't know as you move forward. Just start with what you know (or can guess) and adjust as you go along.

Putting together a business plan is not just some crazy homework assignment. It's a tool to help you build your business and guide you in the right direction. It doesn't have to be a million pages. A couple of pages is fine. It's just a resource for you to get your head straight and lead you in the proper direction.

By the way, if you're thinking of going after investors, your business plan has to be a lot more professional and precise. Most people write a business plan, so they can have somebody invest in their company like an angel investor or a venture capitalist. These people invest in your company and give you money, so you have the capital (cash) to get launched and grow. I'm going to encourage you to *not* do this. As soon as you bring in investors, someone else starts having a say in how things go. You also end up with the additional pressure of trying to protect that person's investment. In my opinion, it's best to try and do whatever it takes to continue to have complete ownership—and control— in your business. As soon as somebody gives you money, they also get control, and before you know it, your company is no longer your company. Instead, I'd suggest you do whatever you have to do, whether it's risking more of your own money or building the business more slowly, to maintain full ownership.

TAKE ACTION #10

Treat each of the following questions like one of your actions exercises. You might want to read through all of them first to get the lay of the land so to speak. Or you can pull out your workbook now and answer each one as you go long. Just make sure you actually do the work!

11 Questions You Need to Ask

We'll break down your business plan by answering eleven different questions. Remember to have your business model where you can see it as you do this because you want to make sure that your plan stays in synch with your vision.

In a business plan, usually the executive summary comes at the beginning. However you need to write the rest of the plan first and write the executive summary last. The executive summary is kind of like when you're reading a book and you open it up to the Table of Contents or the introduction to see what the book will be about. The executive summary is an overview that talks about what problem you're solving and what solution you're offering. It's going to say who your client avatar is and how many of them there are in the market. You'll describe your niche. (I know right now you're thinking you want to reach everybody. But remember the discussion about Russell Brunson's red and blue oceans in the last chapter? If you're able to identify the need of a certain specific group, it will be easier for you to target market your customers who are more likely to buy what you've got.)

So skip your executive summary for now and work through these questions:

Question 1: Who are your customers or clients?

You should have your avatars, your ideal target market, from the work you did on your business model. If not, go back and do it! Once you have your avatars, you need to do a little research. How many of them are there? What are their buying habits? What pushes their buttons and rings their bells? Are they buying things like what you've got already? For example, if you're thinking about a local bricks and mortar fine gift shop, maybe your avatars are women in the 30-50 age range who are upper middle class. Okay, so how many of them are in your area? Where do they currently shop? How much do they spend every year on gifts? Get on Google and other search engines to get as much information as you can.

Here's a crazy thing I learned: You might think you know who your ideal client or customer is. But until you really get into your business, you're not going to know for sure. When I first started my real estate coaching business, I paid a company about $30,000 to help me with my branding. They picked my colors, help me with my business name, and also helped me with my client avatars. Based on their research, I assumed that the client avatar for this new business was a woman between the age of 30 to 45 who had been in the real estate business for a while and made a few deals a year but wanted to do more. Well, I have to tell you that was completely wrong. My client avatar turned out to be a broad group ranging from agents who didn't even have their license yet to people who were selling 90 homes per year. They were not just women. In fact, men were just as attracted to my business model as women.

That said, you still have to start somewhere. So you start by identifying and researching who you think your ideal client would be. Be specific. Find out what things they like and don't like, what they're willing to spend on the type of product or service that you have to offer, where they get their information and recommendations. Then, as you start to build your business, you might find a different group is attracted to your business. Maybe they are in a lower income bracket than you thought so you shift your business plan to include a less expensive option or product. Or maybe you find out that a different age group is interested in what you offer. In that case, you may shift some of your marketing to a vehicle that new group uses to get information. The point is, come up with as good a plan as you can and be flexible!

Question 2: How does your offer benefit them?

In business, this is often called "your unique value proposition." You can come at it by answering a bunch of questions: What problem am I solving for them and how is my solution different? How will their lives be different or better after they buy my product or service? What will they tell their friends about my product or service? What specific benefit will they get that makes them happy to pay the price of my offering? (A specific benefit could be financial, saving or making money. It could be saving time or being healthy and able to live an active life again. Try to come up with something really tangible here.) And once they have received this first benefit, what else can I offer them to make it even better? What new benefits will they get from that new offering?

Let me give you an example in Real Estate. My UVP, Unique Value Proposition, was that I specialized in digital marketing as well as social media target marketing. Most agents had no idea how to market at all, and not a clue as to what digital marketing was. I could easily show the value of social media and how 99% of agents were using it improperly. They underexposed their properties which ultimately cost the sellers thousands and thousands of dollars in net proceeds from the sale. We also included semi-staging of their home, 3-D Virtual tours of all of our properties, etc. etc. I could go on and on about what our unique value proposition was, but I would need an entire chapter! My goal when real estate was my focus was to ensure that my product and service far surpassed my competition. You could see it in everything that I touched and produced within my company.

> "What makes them want to choose you or your service or offering over someone else's?"

What makes them want to choose you or your service or offering over someone else's? Answering this and being able to really pinpoint this could make the difference between your business failing or succeeding. Here's another cool thing to think about, maybe that "thing" that makes your product/service different is YOU, so don't sell yourself short.

Let's look at a few examples, starting with my business when I was just coaching real estate agents. My value proposition or unique value proposition was that I was still selling real estate and I was in the top 1% of agents Nationwide. I was actually implementing all of the techniques and strategies that I taught in my own business and those techniques and strategies were creating huge tangible success for me. Another unique thing was that I was coaching them personally. They were not being coached by someone I had taught. They got me, my experience, knowledge and input. Not only was I a trainer, but I was also a coach, two very different things. I do both well, so they got the best of both worlds.

That was my value add and quite frankly, it was invaluable to them. Learning from my screw ups and successes saved them more time, money and resources than they could have imagined. Experience and previously being in the position of your avatar can be priceless in my opinion.

Another example: I moved into a new home and got quotes from two different companies on window coverings. One of the companies was a bit more expensive, but their customer service was insanely great. The guy who sold me the blinds was also the guy who installed them. He had a true vested interest in his company. He assured me that he wouldn't hire some third- party company to install them, and if there were any problems, he would come out and handle any issues himself. This guy had so much attention to detail, such great customer service, and I could tell that he was passionate about his product and service. I knew that, no matter what happened, I was going to be taken care of. That was his value add, his unique value proposition. I chose him over the other window covering person because I trusted he would take care of me.

This is also where you think about the "red ocean, blue ocean." So ask questions like: Why will my customer or client be happier with what I have to offer over someone else's product or service? How will my service or product stand out, be unique, or resonate more with my clients and customers? How will my product or service meet the specific wants and needs of my client in a better, more efficient, more effective manner than others? How can I add more value to them than others offer?

To answer these questions, you have to do some research to know who your competition is and what they offer. I will admit, I am a student of my competition and you should be too. I have taken their courses, downloaded and saved their emails, watched their webinars, tweeted and changed what they did to make it better and resonate more with my client avatar. This may seem odd to you, but any successful business person will tell you they have a strong pulse on their competition, what they are and are not doing. They mimic and improve on what they can tell is working. Facebook has added a tool on their website and on people's pages called Info and Ads. You can see what ads your competitors are running. My guess is that if they continue to run certain ads for a long time, those ads are probably performing well. Also, you can use programs like AdEspresso, AdLeap or AdSwipe just to name a few.

> "Any successful business person will tell you they have a strong pulse on their competition, what they are and are not doing"

What do your competitors sound like, look like? What do they represent to the market? Based on that information, how will you show up as different? It's called positioning. How are you going to position your product or service in the marketplace? Think of it like this: When you buy a burger, if you go to McDonald's, you can buy a cheeseburger for $.99, right? But if you go to In-N-Out Burger, you can't get a burger for less than five dollars. The difference is low ticket and high ticket or medium ticket. What do you offer that your competitors don't? How are your competitors positioning themselves and what can you do to be different?

Question 3: What specifically are you offering?

We worked through a lot of this in the prior chapters when we talked about your passions and things you're good at and how those might translate into a business. Now is the time to get really nitty gritty about it. For example, say you decided to do webinars on how to write a book. How many webinars? How long will they be? How will you record them? Will you use Power Point or just talk in the camera? Where will you house the recordings? Will people be able to download them, or will they just have access to a site for a limited period? Will you offer printed material along with the webinar? Will they be evergreen or live? Is it just you or are there others involved? What service will you use to do them on and what platform?

Or say you want a bricks and mortar bridal boutique with wedding dresses. Will you offer in-house alterations? Will customers be able to order dresses in other sizes? Will you also have wedding accessories? Will you include bridesmaids' dresses and dresses for mothers of the bride and groom?

Keep in mind that you don't have to offer everything from the start. You can (and should) start small and roll out new offerings along the way. And you may discover something new you want to offer based on how your customers and clients respond. For now, look at your business model and just list as much as you can as specifically as you can about the products or services you can see yourself offering.

> "How are you going to make your clients' and customers' experience exceptional?"

Another big part of what you offer is the customer service side. This is at least as important as the product itself! Think about it: If you go to a dry cleaners who just takes in your clothes, gets them done on time, and charges a reasonable amount, you're okay with it, right? But if you go to a cleaners who remembers your name, always walks your cleaned clothes out to the car, gets your cleaning done really fast if you need it, and offers a rewards program, aren't you more likely to go to them and be loyal even if they charge a little bit more? Absolutely! So think it through: How are you going to make your clients' and customers' experience exceptional?

Let me give you an example, there is a super famous restaurant in very close proximity to where I live. It is difficult to get in, but we knew the rules and we followed them: At this restaurant if you get there before a certain hour, you get 25% off your meal. So we got there one night and waited to be seated. It was unusually busy, so we waited in line for 68 minutes. We were the next to be seated when the manager proceeds to tell us that we did not make the cut. The restaurant was full and we would have to wait for 70 minutes or so to be seated. Like a drill sergeant, she shuffled everyone in line around, telling them they were not properly lining up in line or following procedure.

I was appalled! She was rude, not smiling, showing no appreciation at all for those who had come to the restaurant. This restaurant was so busy and so sought after that they forgot that the customer experience, the way you treat your client and make them feel welcome, far outweighs whatever you're selling. I politely told the manager that I was surprised that they were so successful given the way we were treated. I reminded her that the "customer' her client was truly what made this restaurant succeed. I have to applaud her because she learned from the experience and my constructive criticism. She was gracious for the rest of the evening and made sure we had an amazing experience.

Never, get too busy, or too prideful. Always remember your humble beginnings and that you are meant to serve your client or customer. How you treat them is the bread and butter of your success. You need them more than they need you! If you get to this point in your business where your customers feel like a "nuisance," stop, slow down, and figure out how to serve. I've always said "People before things and the things will always follow." Treat people right, be more concerned with doing the right thing, and the money and success will come.

Question 4: How will your customers and clients find you?

This question is all about marketing and marketing is the key to your success. In fact, the entire second half of this book is about marketing! In my experience, most businesses fail because they don't put enough emphasis on marketing and they don't understand the best ways to market in today's world. Personally, I am a marketing machine. I think marketing all the time because I know it isn't enough to have some terrific product or brilliant book or mind-blowing system. It's like that tree falling in the forest: Who cares if nobody is around to notice it, right?

People can talk about how great your product, service, or idea is. But no matter how amazing it is, if you aren't willing to properly market it, you might as well put this book down. When getting into my business venture, I hired many coaches who were great about helping me figure out what it was that I wanted to sell. But they didn't ever talk about how to market my idea! If you are tempted to go to a workshop or hire a business coach, make sure they are savvy about the marketing aspect and are planning to help you with it. If not, run for the hills! I wasted well over $225,000 working with people who had no clue about how to get my "awesome idea" out into the world!

I'm going to give you a whole of information on marketing in later chapters. For now, try to think about the marketing aspect of your business based on what you know. You can come back later and refine it. As you come up with your marketing plan, I'd recommend *at least* doubling it. In other words, if you think you're going to spend four hours per week and $1000 per month in marketing, make it at least eight hours and $2000. As Grant Cardone said in his book, *10X Rule*, expect everything to take 10 times longer and cost 10 times more money, and require 10 times more resources more people than you ever thought to get where you want to go. Great things don't happen overnight, and they don't happen for free. You are going to have to make an investment. If you're not willing to, put this book down and go back to living your normal life. (Sorry, had to go there. We all need a nasty dose of reality sometimes.)

> "Great things don't happen overnight, and they don't happen for free. You are going to have to make an investment"

Start by thinking about your avatars. Where do they go? How do they get their information? (I'll be talking about internet platforms later and which ones attract the different age ranges. But based on what you know now, give it your best guess.) Who do they listen to and where do they get recommendations for things?

What are their specific hot buttons that you could use in your marketing? For example, FlyLady (the one who built a business around cleaning your house) emphasizes that you don't have to feel overwhelmed in her message. She emphasizes that getting your house under control will help you get your life under control. And isn't that a major hot button for both working and stay-at-home moms? Feeling like our lives are crazy and out of control? What message or copy will get your avatar to stop scrolling on Facebook and read your post or click on your ad on Google or actually open an email they get from you?

Here's a tricky thing about starting a new business: It's usually the time when you have the fewest resources in terms of time and money. But it's also the time when you need to market like crazy! By getting really specific about your avatars and how to target market to them, you'll save yourself a lot of grief—not to mention time and money. Will you market online by using Facebook ads, Google key words, Etsy, and banner ads? Have you set aside a marketing budget for that?

Question 5: What is the cost?

We'll get into other costs like marketing and administration in another question. This one is just about your product or service itself. So if it's a product, how much will the materials cost? How much will it cost to manufacture it? How much on-hand inventory will you need and how will you store it? What are the costs of that? How will you get your product to your customer? Will you ship it yourself or get a fulfillment service? How much would a fulfillment center charge and is it by package or each piece? Will they buy the product or will I? How much will that cost? Will you ship to other countries?

If you're doing something like an eBook or an online webinar, how much will it cost to produce that? Maybe you'll need to have someone format it for you or add graphics. Maybe you'll need to purchase a back drop so your video looks more professional. Maybe you'll have to pay someone to transcribe your video, so you can turn it into an eBook afterwards. If you're coaching, will you send your clients anything in the mail? Will you need an upgraded Skype or Zoom service to connect with them? Will you need to rent hotel space for live presentations or travel to where your clients are? Try to think of all the costs you can and write them down. (Some potential resources for you might be Fivver.com, Freelancer.com, MyOutdesk.com, or for transcription, you can use Rev.com)

Really thinking through the costs of production and distribution can make a huge difference in your business. When I wrote my first book, I ended up losing money on it. The cost of the book itself with all the editing, layout, and design added to the shipping and distribution of the book ended up costing more than I actually made on each book. But I have to say, by writing the book and giving as much information and value to my target market as I could showed them who I was, how I could help, how I was different, and how I resonated with them. It made all the difference in the world. It was well worth it because the book was an avenue for people to get to know me, like me and trust me. It led to getting coaching clients. It also led me to this book and to you, and helped me realize I was meant for a higher purpose. But it did not make money itself. However, if I'd stopped and really thought about it, I could have produced just a digital copy of the book and the outcome would have been very different.

Question 6: How much will you make?

The answer to this is not as simple as "I'll sell my t-shirts!" If you've got a product like that, where will you sell it? Will you wholesale it out or sell it retail directly to customers? Are you focusing on your community and want a small mom 'n pop shop or do you want to sell to the entire city, county, state or nation? How will they be able to pay (cash, credit card, Pay Pal, direct deposit, Stripe)? How much will my processing system allow me to process? Will they shut my account down if I have too many charge backs and returns? How do I minimize chargebacks? Can your bank handle these payments, and do you need to set up a merchant account? What is your return policy? What kind of mark-up will you have over the cost of your product? If you have a sales team, will you hold back part of their commissions to account for chargebacks and returns?

Go through all of these questions and figure out if they apply to your business and how you will handle them. This is important. Some of these seemingly small things can bite you in the butt.

If you have an online-type service like coaching or training, how much will you charge for different offerings? How will clients be able to pay? Do they need to pay all at once or can they make payments? If they make payments will you give them access to the entire course, or will you trickle the course material based upon how much they've paid you? Will you have a money-back guarantee if they aren't satisfied with your course or coaching? If you do offer a money-back guarantee, do they have to do certain things in order to qualify for it, or do they just get a refund automatically. How are you going to monitor that?

Pricing is a huge component layout and positioning. Again think about who your target market is. Do you want to be a McDonald's or In-N-Out Burger? Do you want to be a Target or a Nordstrom? Your pricing is a direct reflection of your avatar, your ideal client or customer. What attracts your avatar initially might be lower priced ticket items. What they buy might change later on once they get to know, like, and trust you and what you offer. The idea is to get them into your funnel (which we discuss more in Chapter 8). Initially, you'll attract a much larger audience if your pricing is more affordable for all. Once they love your product, service, or you, then you can start to have them work their way down your funnel and offer them higher priced items. Think about Costco and their samples. They give you free samples so that you'll like the food and hopefully buy (It also sets up the law of reciprocity, but that's a whole new chapter!). They give you a small taste for free, so you'll enjoy it and want to buy more.

Another huge factor in determining the price is what your competition is charging. Really study your competition. If someone is already doing something really well and they're very successful and charging a certain price, that probably means they've figured out who their avatar is and what price point they're willing to pay. They've matched their goods and services according to that price point. Model your business after what they're doing. There's no reason to reinvent the wheel here. It will cost you more money in the long run if you try to ignore what your competitors are charging. Of course, you also have to compare their value proposition to yours and determine your pricing based upon that difference.

Consider the cost to create what you're offering. Think about the cost of the item itself and all of the things that come along with getting that item to the consumer. (Please know that the fulfillment part, getting what you offer to the customer, is most likely way more than you're thinking. I learned this the hard way!) The cost might actually just be your time and the number of hours you train or coach someone. How much is your time worth? Or how much is your time costing you if you have to take it away from something else? This is why people often create evergreen products, something you create once like a digital product. It keeps your costs of time and money very low.

BTW, your competition might actually be able to help you sell your product by becoming affiliates. An affiliate partner is somebody who offers something similar but not exactly the same as you offer. They can promote your product to their audience and you can promote their product. This can make you both more money. Their audience knows, likes and trusts them, so when they recommend your product, the customer is much more likely to purchase. It's like when a friend gives you a good reference for a restaurant, or any referral for that matter. Many businesses start out in this manner because it saves on marketing cost. Yes, you give that affiliate some of your profits for people who buy because they referred them. But you only pay them when their referral creates a sale. And once you have acquired that customer and have their contact information, you can then upsell to the later, different products.

It's pretty darn crazy because sometimes you'll pay your affiliate partner 100% of the proceeds, but that's okay if it gets you in the door with their connections. A person that comes through an affiliate and buys from you already trusts you because they were referred by a trusted source. Your first sale to them might be something super inexpensive so it doesn't matter if you give 100% of the profits away. Now you'll be able to sell something more expensive to that person who came through an affiliate. Of course, that first product, even if it's inexpensive, still has to be something of real value so you can maintain and expand on the initial trust. You can find all kinds of models for affiliate programs. Just pick your model and stick to it.

> "Never ever promote or advertise a product that you do not believe in or do not know if it really works"

What other products or services could your client avatar use and benefit from? You can't be a jack of all trades. You need to be a master of one. But is there another product, business or service that could be valuable to your client or customer? Find those products and services and see if you can team up and become an affiliate and get paid for promoting them. Many businesses have an entire business model on marketing other peoples or businesses products to their networks and connections. A word of caution: Never ever promote or advertise a product that you do not believe in or do not know if it really works. Don't ever trade money for something that might not give your customer or client great results. Do your research so you don't promote someone who makes you look bad in the end. I'd highly suggest personally using the product or service first to ensure it has value prior to promoting or doing any sort of an affiliate partnership.

Let me give you an example of how important this is. In my coaching program, many of the students became overwhelmed by the technical side of figuring out how to use Facebook ads and campaigns effectively. It is a very important aspect of what I teach but can be seriously difficult for those who aren't tech savvy. So, we interviewed a company to help them implement on Facebook and ended up referring that company to our students before actually using them ourselves. Let me tell you, this was a huge mistake on my part. The company had "talked" a great talk. But when it came down to actually delivering for my students, it was a major disappointment. Of course, I was the one who made the connection so ultimately that disappointment was on my shoulders. Had I experienced the company's process first on my own, I would have seen the warning signs and I would not have made the introduction.

Question 7: What equipment and infrastructure do you need?

If you're planning a teaching or coaching-type business, can you start with your current technology (cell phone, computer, internet service) or do you need to upgrade? Do you have a quiet room in your house with good lighting to create videos or will you have to go somewhere else? Can you make all the calls and "sell the program yourself" or do you need sales associates? Will you pay them on commission or salary plus commission? Will you also pay them on upsells or will that be the responsibility of another department or yourself? Do they get the same split on upsells or is the commission less because they are already a customer? Who will train them? Keep in mind that you can start small and build into something more professional. But you still want the quality of what you offer to be good enough so it's worth what you're charging for it!

For tangible products, what equipment do you need to design and manufacture them? How much space will it take and where will that space be? How will you package your product? Will that take any equipment? What kind of storage space do you need? BTW, Hewlett-Packard started in a garage, so you don't need to go crazy renting space right off the bat!

Question 8: The Hiring Factor?

Even if you wanted to, it's not likely that you'll be able to do everything yourself! So carefully think through the whole process of what you have to offer from producing your offering to getting it to the customer or client to following up with customer service for problems or complaints. What parts do you want others to do and what do you want to handle yourself? What outside services might you need, like an accountant or an editor or a design person? How will you cover vacations or days when you won't be working? What are you good at and what are you terrible at?

Bring in people to help you if you can afford it so you can concentrate on what you're good at and let go of what you have trouble doing. Even if this means that you need to take out a small loan, dig into retirement, ask your parents for a loan, I'd suggest you do it if you can. With people working with you who are good at the part they play, your business will be more efficient and will grow much faster. You are going to need some capital, an initial investment, and you're going to have to continue to invest in order to continue to see growth.

Let's say you've got this great idea for an app that could make people's lives easier, but you're not in any way, shape, or form technically savvy. Do you have the financial resources to hire someone to help you? Do you have the time to figure it out? Do you know other people who could help you? Their strengths might be more technical, but your strength may be understanding the types of problems people have and creative ways to solve them. Are these technical resources located locally or will you reach out to other countries like India or the Philippines?

Like all of the questions, when you think about human resources, you want to think about both, the beginning and after yours is actually running. In the beginning, you may be doing a heck of a lot of this yourself. Maybe you can enlist your kids to help or recruit your spouse. Down the road, you can hire virtual assistants (freelancer.com or fiverr.com) or part-time people to do parts of it.

One thing to consider as you think about human resources is not only how much will it cost you to hire someone but also how much it will cost you to *not* hire someone. How valuable is your time and could you be doing something more productive by hiring help? Could you start generating income from your business sooner if you have people helping? Could you be bringing in more income from another source if someone helped out with your new venture?

I still would caution you about hiring too many people too soon. Be responsible for covering your employees' weekly paychecks can be really stressful on a new business. If you have the extra financial resources to do it, go for it. But if you're relying on your new business to support their salaries, you'd better make sure your cash flow has gotten to the point where it is very steady before making that move.

Give yourself a break here. If you don't have the resources to hire help, just understand that it's going to take you longer to get the results you want. Don't let this distract or discourage you. Go into this new venture with a realistic expectation of how much time is going to take. It's almost always longer than you think! Don't get discouraged but approach it with the right frame of mind. You'll get there. Time is going to pass either way, so don't let the discouragement of how long something may take you keep you from doing it. It will be far more disappointing in the future if you do not start at all.

"Go into this new venture with a realistic expectation of how much time is going to take. It's almost always longer than you think!"

Question 9: What's the Bill & How long will it take?

Notice that the question asks you to start quantifying not only the money your new venture will take but also the *time* it will take. Many people who start a new career or business continue with their old job until the new venture really gets going, this is often smart. Please realize though that if you don't dedicate a good amount of time to your new business, it will never happen. If the time you can devote to it is limited, just be sure to be consistent and know it will take longer for your business to get rolling.

For this question #9, you want to put together two different time and money spreadsheets. (If you aren't a spreadsheet kind of person, just make two different lists that you can add up to get a total, so you get a complete picture of your initial time and money budget.) Your first list or spreadsheet will be all of the time and money costs of just getting started. The second will be the ongoing time and money costs of operation. And I'd recommend that you add at least a 30% "contingency" to each of them! A normal contingency would be 10%, right? But that only works in budgets where you have a track record and know exactly what you're doing. In starting your new venture, you don't! So if you think something will take you 20 hours, assume it will take 26. If you think your new website will cost you $700, budget at least $910.

Your start-up costs will include the production of what you're offering, business license if you need one, additional equipment needed, etc. Your monthly budget will include things like ongoing marketing, fees for internet or web hosting, any paid help, etc. When you've come up with these two budgets, get together with a friend who is business-savvy. Have them take a look at your budgets to see if they think your costs are reasonable or if you need to add any costs you may not have thought of.

Question 10: Reaping Rewards by Mitigating Risks

By now, if you've done the work, you have a pretty complete overview of your business and what it's going to take to get it going. Of course, there will be things you couldn't anticipate but you've got a good foundation. Now you want to look at the risks and rewards.

First, think about what risks are involved and how they might affect you. Don't let risks stop you. What I've learned in my research is that the biggest regrets people have in life are the chances and opportunities that they didn't take that they know they could have. That said, it's important to understand what financial risks could be involved, as well as the amount of time you will invest and how that affects you both personally and financially. Write these risks down. Can you think of ways to mitigate those risks? Ways you can reduce them?

Even more importantly, you want to really think about the rewards. Write down what your life will look like and feel like as you transition into your new venture. What will your life look like and feel like once you've actually reached your goal and are in the middle of where you want to be? This is so important because the real rewards, the gold nuggets are not because of the money you'll make. The true rewards are the satisfaction and joy you get because you're doing something you love, something that makes you happy (Don't get me wrong here, we all love money. But it's what the money actually does for us that counts).

" What I've learned in my research is that the biggest regrets people have in life are the chances and opportunities that they didn't take that they know they could have "

Think about how you are going to measure the success of your company. Is there a certain number of clients you want to reach? Is there a certain amount of money you need to make? Maybe you can measure success based on the amount of time you are able to spend doing what you love. Maybe success is in the amount of positive feedback you get from customers and clients. Use whatever you think of to set milestones and applaud yourself when you've reached them. You need to become your own best cheerleader and to celebrate your wins along the way no matter how small they are.

At the point when I decided to start my coaching and training business, I was doing very well in real estate. Financially I was great, but my bucket was not full. Initially I lost money during the transition. However, because I loved what I was doing, pretty quickly, I was able to make the same amount of money in coaching that I made in real estate. But to get there, I had to risk time, money and make a huge investment of both. I was willing to make the sacrifice because my passion was worth more than my profits. Still it was hard to watch my bank balance dwindle down with all I was investing into the new business. But I kept going and kept pushing on and pretty soon, I struck gold not only monetarily but also personally. I am more fulfilled now than ever and doing what I love, helping and inspiring others.

Question 11: Rolling it Out!

Most business plans will roll out in a sequence rather than trying to make everything happen at once. For example, say you have an overall business model where you want to sell evergreen products, you want to do individual coaching, and you want to make presentations to large groups. Ask yourself, "Where's the easiest place to start? What's the least expensive place to start? And where's the most important place to start?" In your business model, you started with, "What's your ultimate place where you want to end up?" In your business plan, you started breaking down exactly what that means. Now, you need to start figuring out the phases of putting it all together.

For example, my ultimate place where I want to end up, is to be the next Tony Robbins for motivational speaking as a woman. I know that I can't get there instantly, because people have to get to know me. It's not as easy getting asked to speak in front of large audiences as you might think. But it can be done. In fact, by the time this book comes out, I'll be on a plane to Europe talking to people who want to make a change. This came true for me because I am emphatic about my mission— and you need to be too.

So I had to figure out where to start. I'm really an expert in real estate and, though speaking just to real estate people is not my ultimate goal, I realized I could start by using the expertise I had in that industry. So I wrote a book based on real estate. Then I marketed that book as much as I could. Because my goal was to be a public speaker, I started speaking at local events, using the book as my calling card. At first, these events were real estate related but soon I was tapped to speak at other types of events. By building my reputation at smaller, local events, I now get booked at larger events. It just keeps on growing and growing.

My idea of being an author really wasn't because I want to be a bestseller. It's because I needed to have something that gives me credibility and shows that I'm an expert, so that I can actually get on stage to speak. Once I had gotten on stage and was well-received in speaking about real estate, I knew I could recreate that success on a broader level and pretty much speak anywhere.

Take that woman who was in my mastermind class who had a boudoir photography business and wanted to teach other photographers how to have a boudoir photography business. Her ultimate goal was to sell a video course and coach and train individual photographers. Here's how I'd suggest she sequence the roll-out: She could start by creating a small PDF and either giving it for free or charging a very small fee for it. She would do that a couple times so people would get to know her and see the quality of what she was teaching. Next, she might create a series of training videos. She might even give one or two away for free. Each video is on a specific topic like how to make a client feel comfortable during a boudoir photography session, or how to properly position lighting. Once she's given a couple away for free, she can sell the rest of the series. And she can learn how to improve from her beginning clients by asking for feedback or other things they want to learn.

Next, she could create a webinar and invite people who have been interested in her PDF's and videos. She would teach something of value in that webinar then introduce her new course that costs $1,000 and gives a lot more information about boudoir photography and how to succeed at it. Once people have been through the course and see how much it helped them, she can upsell them to a $5,000 course, which teaches them how to take their business model to the very next level. The point is, she doesn't start selling the $5,000 course off the bat because no one's going to buy it. They need to see mini-successes first. They need to be able to get to know that what she's offering works and that it helps before they dive right into buying the big product.

Another example is LadyBoss who sells health and fitness programs to women. She had lost 65 pounds and has been able to keep it off. Her target market is women who want to begin and maintain a healthy weight and lifestyle. She started with her Facebook group (we talk about Facebook groups in a future chapter), constantly giving eating tips, and exercises to do.

Next, she offered a small product. "Here's a mini-workout plan for $27. It shows you how to work out for just 20 minutes a day to help you be able to eat 500 more calories each week, so you don't feel like you're deprived all the time." The people who bought it realized that $27 program works, so she was able to offer them her $1,000 program. Then she up-sold them up to personal video coaching with her that includes group coaching. That's a $4,000 program.

What if you want to open a bridal boutique but don't have the resources to open up a big store right away? You could start by getting a booth at bridal fairs and bringing your merchandise there. You could start by showing some of your dresses online on Facebook, and have people come in to your garage or a room in your house to purchase them. Then maybe you could approach a store owner and say, "Hey, can I just rent one fifth of your store?" Rather than making a big commitment with your own store, you can rent a small space from someone else's store. Once people get to know you and the word gets out that you have great stuff, then you can consider opening your own store.

Let's say you want to teach how to live a pain-free life and your ultimate goal is to work with people one on one or in small group settings (which could be costly). You can start out by doing a few free online classes or videos that you pump out teaching techniques to help people be pain-free (or have less pain). Then you could invite them to join a free Facebook group where you give free tips and strategies to help alleviate pain, like changing their diet, changing their posture, or doing certain exercises. Eventually, you could invite the free group to enroll for your monthly program where you give more personalized tips and exercises where they also have direct access to you and what you provide.

Take some time and look at your new business. How can you get it started? What are some different stages and what sequence can you put them in?

Executive Summary

You're getting this right? Not just as easy as "Oh I have a great idea and I want to get it into the world." But don't let these questions freak you out. Let them help you see what you need to be prepared for and how to plan appropriately. So let's put it all together in an executive summary. This will be a fill in the blank exercise based on your answers above. If you're not clear yet on how to fill in any of the blanks, just pencil something in. But highlight it so you will go back and do the research or whatever you have to do to complete it.

1. The name of my new business is _________________________. I will be offering ___________________________.

2. My clients or customers are (briefly describe them) ________________. They are located ______________________. There are approximately (give a number) ____________________________ people in this niche.

3. What my clients need and want is ___________________. The benefits I will bring to my clients are _________________________.

4. My competitors include _________________________________. I stand out from them because ________________________________.

5. Specifically, what I am offering is ______________________________ and it takes the form of ____________________(like personal coaching or eBooks or a product).

6. My potential customers or clients get information and referrals by __________________ (internet, word of mouth, etc.) I will market my business by ______________________________. (We get into marketing in much more depth in later chapters. Just fill in your ideas for now.)

7. The cost to produce or create what I offer is ____________________. (Itemize each offering).

8. The ways I will make money from my business include _______________.

9. The human resources I will use are __________________________.

10. My budget for the launch of my business is ______________. Ongoing annual expenses should be ___________________. My time budget for the launch will be ______________________. My time budget after the launch will be _________________________.

11. The different stages of rolling out my business will be #1 ____________#2_____________________ #3___________________ (write as many stages as you want)

12. The major risks of starting this business are _________________. I will lessen these risks by ________________________________.

13. The important rewards I intend to reap are __________________.

That's it! Pat yourself on the back for all your hard work in creating this plan. Now go back and do whatever you need to do to make your plan more complete because next we'll break down the specific action steps you need to take and how to organize yourself to get this great business launched!

CHAPTER SIX

Just Do It!

So you've figured out, "Okay, here's what I want." You also went through a planning process, so you have a good idea of what you need in resources and the specific phases for launching your business. Next you need to ask yourself, "What specific steps am I going to take starting right NOW to get there? How persistent am I going to be to make sure I follow through with this?" You can want whatever you want. Having a great desire and a good attitude is awesome. But remember, if you don't take action, nothing's going to happen. Learn (you've just learned), Implement (now it's time to implement), Master (get really good) and then Repeat!

"Having a great desire and a good attitude is awesome. But remember, if you don't take action, nothing's going to happen"

Just start. You don't have to be perfect.

Whether you start taking action now, or start a year from now when everything's perfect, you're still going to have to change things and modify what you're doing as you get further into it. You don't know what you don't know. Even though you think you can anticipate everything, you can't. Even though you think you're giving your clients or customers exactly what they want, you'll find out that you're missing something. Even though you think you're doing it all the right way, you never are because it's a whole new thing for you. You don't know what you don't know. While you're waiting to make it perfect, you don't even know what perfect is or isn't. The only way you find out is by just starting.

When I first had my idea about becoming a coach and public speaker, I had already mastered the real estate industry. I still love real estate and plan to continue to do it and stay involved in it. But I was at a point in my life where I realized, "Hey, I think I'm meant for more." I knew my passion was teaching and coaching so I came up with a business model. Honestly, I hadn't really stopped to come up with a clear plan—so you're already ahead of me!—but I jumped in anyway.

I wanted to get better at public speaking, so I hired a speaking coach right away. I spent a bunch of money (that I drew from my real estate business) on this speaking coach. It didn't feel the greatest. I just wasn't ready for her. I didn't even know what I was going to talk about, so I basically put her on hold for nine months.

Then, I hired another coach and joined a program. I just kept going to trainings on how to build a coaching business, how to be a great speaker, and all kinds of different trainings. One person contradicted what the other person said. I got so many ideas of what to do that I found it hard to implement anything. So, I realized I had to slow down, implement what I was learning prior to jumping into another training or hiring another coach.

Then I thought, "My new business is going to explode so fast, I want to make sure that, when I do, my brand is perfect." So I hired a branding specialist. We spent four months and $30,000 just developing my brand. It's all great stuff. But although I think it's important to have a brand, I didn't need to spend the amount of money and time I did on it. At the end of the day, it doesn't really matter if the font is Century Gothic or GungsuhChe (Yes, that really is a type of font!). Using aqua versus periwinkle in your logo won't make or break you. The branding work was helpful, but it did not propel me forward.

I went to another training and created a webinar that was supposed to encourage people to buy my product, even though I didn't even have a product to sell yet. I was creating a marketing webinar without a product and I never even launched it. It was all backwards. I did everything backwards without knowing it. Then, literally a year and a half later, as I was creating another marketing webinar, I realized, "Wow, why am I even doing this?"

I should have just started on a smaller level. Then, as I started growing, finding out what my people needed and wanted and how I could best help them, I could start incorporating more as I went along. I needed to stop and think about how to just simply start, without investing a lot of money and time. Then after mastering that small level, I could take it to the next level.

I finally figured it out and just said, "Screw it, I'm starting with what I've got." I stopped worrying whether my picture was right or if my logo looked good. That's when I really started to grow and learn. In fact, a few months after I just started, I realized that the logo and company name I had spent so much time and money creating couldn't even be used! It conflicted with another company's name and logo. So I dropped it. And mind you I had created about forty professional videos using the logo that I couldn't use

But it didn't stop me. I kept pushing forward. I kept pushing out content. I just adjusted it and modified it as I went on and as I had the budget to do it. I just kept going. I just used my own name. I just called it Krista Mashore Coaching, and it was just fine. In the very beginning, if I had taken these simple steps I started to take rather than spending time getting the perfect branding and doing so much training, I would be so much further than I am now.

I don't want you to make that same mistake. You've worked through your business model and thought through your business plan. Now is the time to get started in a way that makes sense based on the time and resources you have. It won't all happen at once. You'll take specific action steps one step at a time. As you start setting specific goals, go back to the last chapter and the work you did on Question 11 about the sequence to roll out your business. Your first action steps and initial goals will follow that sequence (though, of course, it will change as you get deeper into it and learn more).

> "It won't all happen at once. You'll take specific action steps one step at a time"

Sacrificing for the Sake of Success

Setting goals is incredibly important in starting a new career or business. A goal is a specific result you want to create. So a goal might be, "I create one hundred t-shirts to sell at the county fair on September 15th, 20XX." That's a good, clear goal. Doesn't it make some of your specific action steps obvious? You need to design the shirts. You need to buy equipment to produce the shirts. If you are putting your design on already-made shirts, you need to order them. You need to apply for a spot at the fair and, if you're making the t-shirts from scratch, you better get sewing!

You need both long term (like five years) and short term (monthly and weekly) goals to keep you moving forward. If you just set long term goals, you won't be as motivated to complete them. When something is too far out in the future, you feel no urgency to get it done. If you're like most people, you'll just keep putting off doing anything about it. Weekly and monthly goals will keep you accountable and keep you focused.

The other thing about short term goals is that they give you wins along the way. Remember, this is a marathon, not just a sprint. Your ultimate vision of what you want to create won't happen overnight so you need to have smaller, short term goals so you can feel like you're getting somewhere and gaining on it.

> "Remember, this is a marathon, not just a sprint"

I start by laying out my monthly goals. On a 3 X 5 card, I write: "By the end of the month I will have accomplished these primary objective/goals." Then I fill in the weekly goals for the month: "Within the first week I will have accomplished X, Y, Z." Then I do this for the 2nd, 3rd, and 4th week so that by the end of the month my macro (larger) goal is complete. Write down your goals for each week. Write down the specific action steps that you need to take that will get you there. Thus, by the end of the month, you have completed a huge step toward where you want to go, and you'll feel that sense of accomplishment.

It's very important to have daily goals. Each day write down 3-5 things that you absolutely must get done. When you get them done, pat yourself on your back and celebrate your success. Remember, small successes breed more success, so give yourself kudos where kudos are due. Don't forget to look back on all you've accomplished as you're accomplishing it. Be appreciative of what you have done today.

Please try NOT to beat yourself up if you are not able to get done what you hoped to accomplish. Things come up that take precedence and priority over your goals. Just move that goal over to the next day, week, or month and pat yourself on the back for all you've accomplished. Just pay attention to those goals so that you're always moving to the next week or month. Are they really necessary? Do you need to buckle down and just push through them? Or do you need help of some kind to get them done?

Remember, we're in a marathon, not a sprint. As they say, Rome wasn't built in a day, right? Your business will take time as well. I made the huge mistake of thinking I could reinvent and change my career within six months. (Yes, that actually was my goal!) It took me a year and four months to launch, and it was only a mini launch. The true launch took around 26 months. It's going wonderfully and I'm loving it, but it took way more time, way more resources and way more energy than I had anticipated, yes, I realized I wasn't Super Woman. You should anticipate that too. Creating a long lasting business that you love and look forward to doing everyday isn't always easy nor is it fast. So just prepare yourself for it. It's better to take a year or two getting where you want to go instead of looking back in ten or eleven years wishing you had just started and paid the price back then.

TAKE ACTION # 11

As you start laying out specific goals and action steps, take a moment to think about what you'll need to change in your current lifestyle. You need to give up something to get something you want more, right? If you want to lose forty pounds, you'll probably have to give up daily hot fudge sundaes. If you want to build a successful business, you'll probably have to give up binge-watching the latest Hulu series. I call these "smart sacrifices" because you are consciously choosing what you will give up for now, so you can create the life you really want down the line. "Dumb sacrifices" are things like compromising your health or jeopardizing your important relationships. These are things entrepreneurs often sacrifice for success only to wake up one day and realize they've lost what is most important in life. You don't have to do that. You can be smart about it and keep your priorities straight. Maybe you'll sacrifice eating out as often, so you can pay an assistant to help you. Maybe you'll wake up a half an hour earlier to work on your business. Maybe you'll play golf less often or pack a lunch, so you can work during your lunch hour. Take a few moments right now to journal about what you're willing to give up to have the time and energy you need for your new business.

Taking the First Step

If you're a person who aims high in life and I've done my job in writing this book, you're probably eager to get started on the path to turning your passion into your new career and reaping all the benefits that go with it. Good for you! To start, it's important to understand how to set effective goals so when the going gets a little tough—which it will—you have the juice to keep going to achieve what you're after. It takes work to get what you want, but you can do anything you put your mind to.

I've always been the kind of person who decides what she wants and goes for it. I was setting goals long before I really knew how to do it. My goals—and my determination to achieve them—have helped me create an incredible business and a really satisfying personal life. I'd like the same for you. I've studied a lot of different goal-setting systems and taken what I think is the best from each. If your goals have produced mediocre results so far, it might be due to the specific *way* you're setting goals. Or it may be due to the fact that you're setting goals that are unrealistic. Dream big but take small steps.

Ready, Aim, FIRE

In working with goals, you have to begin with the big picture before you narrow it down into smaller goals and tasks. It's that clear vision of what you ultimately want in all the areas of your life that you created in Chapter One. If you skipped the work and didn't put together your vision in Chapter One, I'd really suggest that you go back and do it now. That vision you wrote, that ultimate result in each area, is where you want to aim. The next level of goal-setting is about how you're going to get there.

For example, back to the t-shirt example. A guy who wants to create and sell t-shirts might have a vision that sounds like: I have a highly successful business where I make t-shirts with sayings that inspire people. I am able to earn $80,000 per year and still give $12,000 per year to my favorite charity. I have a small shop where we produce the t-shirts that employs twenty formerly homeless people. I work four days per week so I have time to spend with my kids and can coach their sports teams.

He probably has more detail in his vision but that reflects his ultimate goal, of where he wants to aim. Next, he needs to create specific goals that show how and when he'll accomplish the steps he needs to get there. For example, his one- year goals might include "Sell one thousand units by December, 20XX" and "Hire and train three people through the County Services program by December, 20XX." If he's going to meet those goals, it's now clearer what he needs to do in the next week and the next month, right? His vision is still where he's aiming but his specific goals give him concrete steps to take along the way. They are like the roadmap to get where he ultimately wants to go.

Making It Real

A goal is a specific result you want to achieve and it's one of the steps toward getting your ultimate vision. Your vision may make you feel all warm and fuzzy, but if you don't set specific goals for getting there, it will remain a pleasant dream—and end up being a regret later!

> "Your vision may make you feel all warm and fuzzy, but if you don't set specific goals for getting there, it will remain a pleasant dream—and end up being a regret later!"

One of the cool things about setting goals correctly is that it gets your unconscious mind on board and working for you. When you keep a good goal in mind, even without your knowing it, your brain gets involved in figuring out how to get there. Back in 1960, Dr. Maxwell Maltz, wrote a great book called *Psycho-Cubernetics*. After reading this book, I realized that most great leaders and teachers today are actually saying what he said long ago—and that others said the same thing even before he did! Basically, Dr. Maltz wrote that your mind works to get you exactly what you want. If you create a mental picture in your mind, then visualize and see yourself in that picture in the present, the mind will help get you there. Your central nervous system does not know the difference between what's real and what's not. There is a lot of research to back this up.

When you set a good goal, that's exactly what you are doing. You are giving your mind a clear picture. A lot of the teachers I've studied with and authors I've read use the acronym SMART to remind us how to set good goals.

Here's a quick breakdown of what SMART stands for.

S: The S stands for specific. You need a clear target. Say, your vision is that you make $150,000 per year from your business. Great! Now how much are you going to make in the first year? How are you going to make it? Your goal might be, "By January, 20XX, I am selling four hundred t-shirts per month and putting my profits of $2000 per month back into the business." Actually, a goal to make a profit then re-invest it in your business is sometimes a good idea! But see how specific that is? From there, you would know exactly what goals to set for the next week or month, right?

M: The M stands for *measurable*. If you can't measure your goal, how will you know when you've achieved it? Some goals are tricky to measure. Think of it this way: What will prove to you that you achieved that goal? The t-shirt guy might have a goal to "Get a good marketing campaign going." Okay, but what will it take to prove that? A better goal is "I place ongoing ads on Facebook to my target audience and create a Facebook group page by April 15, 20XX." Now he'll be able to tell if he's accomplished his goal or not.

A: A stands for *achievable*. *Achievable* means that on some level you believe you can reach this goal. It might be (and actually should be) a stretch, not something that is a no-brainer for you. It should take some effort and focus on your part. But, if in your heart, you really don't believe you can reach your goal, it's unlikely you'll really go for it. Take your "impossible" goal and just back off a notch. The t-shirt guy might think that hiring and training ten people by the end of the year is too difficult and risky. So he could set his goal for two people, and when he reaches it, he can ratchet it up.

R: The R stands for *realistic*. A lot of seemingly impossible things really are possible. The question is whether it's realistic to expect that end result for you at this time given who you are and what you know. Maybe you need more training, or maybe you need more help than you have. If that's the case, set those things as your first goals. For example, maybe the t-shirt guy needs some coaching from County Services about how to hire and train homeless people, so he feels confident in dealing with their issues. He could set a goal to get that training before he starts hiring.

Part of what sometimes makes a goal seem unrealistic is that it conflicts somehow with your overall life. It's important that you not screw up your personal life or your health by setting crazy goals. The t-shirt guy might realize that he could hire and train ten people in a year but only if he worked crazy hours and used his life savings to make sure they got paid. Don't get me wrong. You will have to make some sacrifices along the way. Just make sure that the sacrifices you make don't create massive problems for you in other areas of life.

T: The T is for *time.* A goal without a timeframe is meaningless. "Someday" never comes. What if you got to pay your taxes "someday" rather than April 15th? Would you even do it? When you have a specific deadline, you know how much energy you need to put into it. Think about it. Say, the t-shirt guy said, "I am selling one thousand t-shirts per month within the next three months" versus "I am selling one thousand t-shirts per month five years from now." The three- month goal would require a heck of a lot more hustle than the three year goal, right? When you set a timeframe, it's easy to organize yourself and set your priorities.

A couple of other pointers about goals:

1. They should always be written in present tense. Again, it's so your unconscious mind is clear about its job. If you say, "I *am going to* do this or that," your unconscious mind is off the hook. It thinks, "Okay, well, that's in the future. I don't have to worry about it." If you say, "I am doing this or that," your unconscious mind says, "Uh oh. I'd better get moving on this!"

2. Your goals should make sense and be meaningful to you. Say, you have someone telling you that you really should order your t-shirts from China, but you don't want to. Or that you should hire students rather than homeless people. If that advice doesn't resonate with you, don't make it a goal! This is your life and your business. Set goals where you can clearly say, "Yep. That's a good step toward what I really want."

3. Keep your goals simple. It's better to have a bunch of different goals than one goal that takes up twenty paragraphs! If you make it too complicated, you won't know where to start. For example, Mr. T-shirt would know exactly what steps to take on a goal of "I produce and sell 400 t-shirts at local fairs by December, 20XX." Based on this, he knows that he needs to design the shirts, order the blank shirts, get equipment, make 400 shirts, find local fairs, register for them, get a booth etc. He can put dates and set deadlines for each of those micro goals and may have sub-goals that go under some of them like "research best equipment." But if his goal was, "By December 20XX, I sell 400 t-shirts of different colors and sizes that have inspirational sayings on them from world leaders by going to the fair in Los Gatos and the one in Merced and the other fair in Oakland and I have a booth that is built of PVC and has a tarp over it that . . ." Yikes! Too complicated! Your mind would go nuts trying to figure out what comes next. Make your goal simple and add all that other stuff into tasks and sub-goals with their own dates.

TAKE ACTION # 12

Look at your vision again and review the part that is about your new business. Review your business model and plan. Then go to your workbook. You'll set short-term (within 3 months), mid-term (6 to 12 months), and long term (over a year) goals. Once you have these down, you can start creating monthly and weekly goals. But it's often clearer to start long-term then back up into shorter-term goals that support it.

Don't just keep your goals in your head! Write them down, making sure they are SMART goals. Even if you have no idea how to achieve a goal, write it down and think about it every day.

See Where You Are To Know Where To Go

To transition from where you are now to where you want to be, the keys are focus and time management. Start by laying out what your days look like now. Write down your day. What does your typical work day look like? Your typical week? Your typical weekend? How you spend your time now becomes your baseline. Literally, write it down. It might look something like this:

Weekdays	6:30-8:30	Get dressed, get kids ready for school, fix lunches
	9:00-12:00	Work at office
	12:00-1:00	Lunch hour (yoga M-F)
	1:00-5:00	Work (Wed. 1:00-3:00 volunteer at school)
	5:30-7:30	Make dinner, help kids with homework
	7:30-9:30	TV time; kids to bed
	9:30-10:30	Catch up on Facebook, read emails
	10:30	Head to bed

Using this example, if you wake up every day at 6:30 A.M. because you need to be at work by 9:00, can you wake up earlier? Maybe at 5:00? This would give you an extra hour and a half to work on your new business. Or maybe you only work out 2-3 days during the week, so you have an extra 2-3 more hours. You can work out on the weekends if exercise is a priority. Even if you're not a morning person, and you hate getting up, are you willing to do it anyway to pursue your passion? You've got to make sacrifices somewhere. You've got to do something different because, if you keep doing what you've always done, nothing is going to change. You have to figure out what you can change in your life to get from point A to point B.

> "You've got to do something different because, if you keep doing what you've always done, nothing is going to change"

So maybe you decide to wake up an hour or two hours earlier. Next, what about your lunch hour? (BTW, I *never* recommend that you use your employer's time to work on your new business! That's actually stealing, and you won't feel good about it.) So if you have an hour lunch, during that hour, you can spend 15 minutes eating then use the next 45 minutes researching or mapping out your next action steps. Maybe you use some of your time on the weekend to prepare lunches and dinners, for the week so you can spend that time during the work week studying or working on your business model.

What about your evening hours? In the example above, maybe you skip TV and Facebook time. Maybe you stay up an hour later. If you have kids, you can put the kids to bed then spend the rest of the evening on your new venture. You may have to try different scenarios to see what's going to work for you. Some people are sharper in the morning and others come to life at night. Even in those hours where you're not at your most brilliant, you can still get something done toward your new business.

Look, I know everyone's busy. I am one of the busiest people I know, and I still make time. I'm running two companies. I have a husband and I've got kids. I volunteer, and I have my own non-profit organization to work with teens. But I still make time to continue building my business because coaching and training people is my passion. I really know where I want to be, and I know that I won't have to work this hard forever. When a rocket gets launched into outer space, they say that the part that takes the most fuel and energy is the very beginning when the rocket is breaking through the atmosphere. Starting your business is like launching a rocket. You have to commit a ton of energy and time to get it launched.

Put in the sweat equity now so that in a few years you can sit back and reap the rewards. You need to do something different today than you did yesterday and years previous to create a different outcome tomorrow. Getting what you want takes time and work, but the rewards will be more beneficial than you can imagine. Just Do IT!!!

"Put in the sweat equity now so that in a few years you can sit back and reap the rewards"

TAKE ACTION #13

Sit down with your workbook and write down your current normal schedule. Now, how could you tweak it, what could you do differently to make time for your new venture? Be realistic. You need to stay consistent with your plan. Deciding, "I'll go to bed at midnight and get up at 3:30 everyday" probably won't be sustainable. Look first at your time-wasters (Sorry, I've got to put surfing Facebook in this category!) and things you now do that someone else could do or help with (Could the kids start doing their own laundry? Could you start ride-sharing with other moms to cut down on kid-taxi time?) What could you do more efficiently? Write it all down then calculate how much time that gives you each week and each month to work on your new business.

Putting it All Together

Place your vision and goals on your bathroom mirror, tape them to your laptop screen, or put them in a place that you go to frequently. Every time you see these goals, I want you to remember *why* you want those goals. Read them every morning when you wake up and every night before you go to sleep. Out loud is best. I even speak them into my iPhone so I can listen to them as often as I can whenever I have a minute.

I also like to create vision boards. This isn't for everybody, but visuals often help. I get poster board and find pictures in magazines of what I'm going after then write titles on them. I might use a family on a beach and write "Hawaii, May, 20XX" on it. Or I could use a picture of a big audience and write, "Speaking engagement for 500 people by January, 20XX." Whenever I look at my vision boards, I stop and imagine how great it feels to have accomplished these things.

TAKE ACTION #14

Next, get going and take action on your goals! Make a deal with yourself that every day you will take at least one step, big or small, to move closer to that goal. Having a dream without clearly written goals is just a fantasy. And **a goal without action behind it is just fiction.** Schedule your action steps on your calendar for at least the next month. If you aren't sure what steps to take specifically right now, still schedule in a time to do something toward your goals.

> "Having a dream without clearly written goals is just a fantasy. And **a goal without action behind it is just fiction**"

Think about it: If doing something is important to you, it shows up on your calendar, right? If your goals are important to you, the steps toward them need to show up on your calendar too. Heck, they are at least as important as that appointment to get your teeth cleaned! Too often, we put our dreams and goals on the back burner. If you want your new business to really come true, you've got to make it a priority.

Action steps you take toward your goals don't have to be huge, but they do need to be consistent. For example, you may have a goal to "Create a website to sell my product online by December, 20XX." You might start by looking at websites for businesses that are similar to yours and noticing how they are structured. Next, you might research different payment systems for purchases online. You might contact a local community college to see if they have students who can create websites inexpensively. You might take pictures of your product to upload to it or write some blogs that will be on the site. Whatever it is, just make sure you take a step closer to your goal every day.

If you want to get where you want to be, you have to make sacrifices. If you're not willing to make sacrifices, then it's just not going to happen. You have to make educated decisions and choices. You have to make the commitment to yourself. You have to love yourself enough (or maybe you have to dislike the situation you're in enough) that you're determined to make it happen. You have to be so excited about where you're going to go, that you know, "I'm going to do this no matter what."

"If you want to get where you want to be, you have to make sacrifices. If you're not willing to make sacrifices, then it's just not going to happen"

Follow your passions and go after your dreams, don't let yourself down, or you're going to look back with regret that you didn't even give it your best shot. When people look back at their lives, they have the most remorse and the most regret and the most sorrow over things they know they could have done, and didn't. It's not the things you can't control that you'll regret the most. It's the things that you have control over that you didn't take control of. It's the opportunities you let just pass you by and the openings you didn't act upon, even though you know you should have. The past is the past. Focus on right now. If you know you still can follow your passion but don't do it, that's when you'll have the most regret.

"It's not the things you can't control that you'll regret the most. It's the things that you have control over that you didn't take control of"

Quitting Your Day Job

One big mistake people often make is they quit their day job too soon. They want to go for it, and they end up putting themselves under tremendous stress. I have two philosophies on that.

One of my philosophies is, "Hey, take the time. It might take you double and triple the amount of time to get there by working on your business just a few hours per day. But you can still get there." For most people, this is the way they need to begin. They have responsibilities and financial obligations so jumping away from what helps them pay the bills to start something new would be way too stressful for them.

My other philosophy is that sometimes the only way to really figure it out is to have your feet to the fire and jump right in. It just depends upon what kind of person you are. There are so many stories where very successful people admit, "Hey, I realized that I just had to hit rock bottom, lose everything, and have nothing to fall back on, so I would finally do this." I'm not telling you when to quit your day job and move into your new career full time. It works differently for different people.

Personally, when transitioning this time I still worked my real estate business. Number one, I love it. Number two, I needed the money to build and create my new business. Number three, it dovetails with the new career I'm building. Everything I learned in my real estate business, I used in my coaching business. So for me, they're kind of one and the same. And based on my financial responsibilities, there's no way that I would be able to just quit real estate and go straight into coaching full time. That said, I've rearranged my real estate business and my personal time so that I can give my new business most of my energy and focus.

However, the very first time I transitioned into a new career—from teaching to real estate—I didn't have the option to take it slow and keep one foot in my old career. I had nothing in the bank, a mortgage to cover and two little girls to support. Talk about feet to the fire! I was under a heck of a lot of stress. I absolutely had to succeed in my new real estate career. I turned that that stress into determination to be the best and provide for my daughters. The result was that I broke all kinds of records in my very first year.

So one philosophy is, "Go All In," and the other one is, "Hey, take your time, but make sure you've got the tenacity to stick it out for the long haul." Again, please remember and hear me out on this: It is going to take you way more time, energy and resources than you are planning. It's just the way it is, so incorporate that into what you're planning. I don't say that again to be negative but to give you proper expectations so that you plan accordingly for it and don't beat yourself up when things go awry, because they will. When they do, just keep pushing and you'll end up fine in the end.

Remember, if you don't have the resources, and you have to still keep your job, you have to figure out a schedule. Sit down and think, "Okay, how am I going to be able to fit all this in?" Make yourself a schedule then stick to it. For some people, this will be, "Okay, my job is from nine to five, and usually I wake up at 7:00. Maybe I can wake up at 5:00 every day. That'll give me two more hours." So they work on their new business from 5:00 to 7:00, or maybe it's even 4:00 to 6:00. That schedule gives you an additional ten hours during the work week. If normally you wind down at eight o'clock and watch TV for a couple of hours before going to bed, instead of doing what you normally do, spend that two hours dedicated toward your new business. By adding two hours in the morning and two in the evening, you've given your business twenty hours in every work week.

You can also dedicate some time on the weekends. But I'll tell you, one of my biggest challenges is still that I don't stop enough. I will just work all weekend because I really enjoy what I'm doing. I feel like it's my hobby. But your brain needs a refresher sometimes. When we went to Hawaii a while back, I was in a different time zone, so I was waking up at 2:00 in the morning. I got up and worked from 2:00 until 7:00 or 8:00 in the morning the whole time I was there. I enjoyed it, but looking back now, that wasn't smart of me to do. Your brain needs a refresher and your family needs your time. I had my nose in my laptop for hours. People even came up to me in the pool area and said, "Are you by yourself here? All you're doing is working!" I thought, "Oh, my gosh!" I felt like a jack ass!

I look back at that and I regret it. I should have been cuddling with my husband, even though he was sleeping. I should have been giving my body and my mind the time to relax. When you have a chance to refresh, you can think of new ideas and not get so stagnant. Be sure to take care of yourself along the way.

Just Jump In

So I went straight from being a teacher for six years to jumping into real estate. I had planned for a slower, easier transition but suddenly my husband left me, and I had to support myself and my two children. I didn't have time to waste in trying to be perfect. I just jumped right in knowing, "I have got to make this happen!"

My friend Heather just jumped into writing screenplays. She had already figured out that her passion was writing, and she'd made a career out of writing a few novels and doing a lot of ghostwriting. But she always thought it would be fun to write scripts for movies. She read a couple books on it and read a whole bunch of good scripts. Then just jumped in and started writing her own screenplays, trying to follow the guidelines. It took her a while to write her first one. When she finished it, she did some research on how to market it. She didn't want to do all the things people suggested, like move to LA but she did a few things that made sense to her. She ended up posting the script on this online site for screenwriters. In less than a year, it was bought by an LA producer. Now, she's going back and taking a course to figure out how to really write a screenplay.

The point is that she's a lot farther along today because she just jumped in. She learned a heck of a lot by working with a real live producer on a script, and now, a lot of what she's learning in the course on screenwriting makes much more sense to her. She's a lot happier too.

Remember, you need to make up your own mind based upon the type of person that you are and what feels comfortable for you, on what the best scenario for you is to start. These are just suggestions and recommendations and not set in stone. Starting and taking action is the key!

> "It's like getting pregnant. There is never a perfect time and you can never be totally prepared!"

Tonya is a real estate agent and Chrissy worked in the business world. They just weren't happy. So, they decided to start a business making t-shirts. They did their own research and bought a $400 heat press. They searched on Goggle to figure out what the t-shirt market was like and who their potential customers would be. They asked some questions from friends who had similar businesses. They learned a little bit about marketing. Then they just started.

They made some mistakes along the way. For example, since they were both still working, they hired a lady and paid her $4,000 to help with their social media campaigns. They didn't really have the resources to do that, and the woman did not work out in the end. They finally realized that they had to learn about social media themselves. They had to do the work on their social media campaigns and marketing on weekends and in the evenings until they could really afford to outsource the work.

They're still in the process of growing the business but they are making sales. And, hey, once you make one sale, you know you can make more, right? Their business is definitely farther along, even with all their mistakes, then it would be if they had waited until "the time was right." It's like getting pregnant. There is never a perfect time and you can never be totally prepared!

Evolving as You Go

Your passion and your business will evolve as you evolve. When Natalie was younger, she was into fitness. As her life changed and as she became more interested in other things. She changed her brand and the audience she was targeting as she changed and grew. She totally changed who her target audience was based upon the experiences she was going through. She took all she had learned from being a personal trainer and put it into a business called Modern Mom Lifestyle.

Remember the story about peeing your pants on national TV? That's Natalie. She made millions of dollars on her little $27 eBook on how to not pee your pants. Then she realized that an audience of moms was drawn to her because she had helped them with a really embarrassing problem. She realized that she could capitalize on this and address other mom problems.

Now she teaches moms how to be a mom in today's day and age and still have a life for themselves. For example, she teaches tricks on how to do your makeup in five minutes or less. She has a slow cooker recipe book and shows moms how to prepare quick and healthy meals. She has just under 500,000 followers on her Facebook group and she constantly gives them information and gives value, then upsells to them with various eBooks and even healthy supplements. The point is it starts from one thing and it goes so much further.

Francel is a physical therapist and a nurse who has a passion for helping people. She knows that nurses are under a lot of stress. The thing about nurses and doctors is that they don't really seek help for their problems. Of all professions, doctors have the highest suicide rate, and rank high in alcoholism and drug addiction. They have a lot of anxiety and are stressed out. Many of them have tons of pressure on them and they have nowhere to turn. Yet, if they ask for help, they get chastised for it. And nurses are the same.

Francel worked for herself as a Doctor of Chiropractic and a registered nurse. She was doing okay but not as well as she could because she didn't market herself properly. She also had a passion to help nurses because they have nowhere to turn. I helped her completely develop her business model and plan her transition. She set up her Facebook page, set up her Twitter page, did her business makeover, and learned social media. She now does videos that help nurses deal with the stresses of their lives and helps them create a better quality of life for themselves. Her videos focus on how to take care of yourself while taking care of everyone else. For example, one is about how to maintain the right posture or regularly do certain exercises to help you withstand the pressure of lifting your patients. The videos not only help nurses but also encourages them to get to know her. If they need additional help and her services, they'll be comfortable reaching out to her because of the trust factor created in the videos.

The point is just begin where you are with what you know. As you grow and learn, your business will change and evolve with you. Please remember you don't have to wait until that time. Get started now!

TAKE ACTION #15

Look at your goals and look at the time you've set aside to work on them. Now brainstorm steps you can take. Maybe it's researching part of your business online or by interviewing someone who might need your product. Maybe it's getting clear on costs for putting up a website or making your product. Maybe it's checking into virtual assistants to help with certain parts of your business. Maybe it's making a few prototypes of your product or clearing a space in your garage to keep inventory. Try to come up with a month's worth of action steps you can take. After you've thought of as much as you can, schedule those specific steps into your calendar. Now start doing them and checking them off!

CHAPTER 7

What Does "Entrepreneur" Really Mean?

There is no quick fix and no bullet train to the success you want. During my journey I paid hundreds of thousands of dollars (yes, that much) hiring coaches, and specialists and, while they were all helpful, it still took time. It took persistence, consistency, dedication and continuing to educate, learn, implement, master, repeat and tweak what I was doing until it worked. Then once it worked, I still had to go back to the drawing board because things change.

> "There is no quick fix and no bullet train to the success you want"

But from my experience and the mentors I've had, I've learned massive amounts of valuable information. I want to share a few of the secrets to becoming a successful entrepreneur I learned along the way:

One Thing at a Time

Learning from others is really important. But the most important thing is to find one person, or coach, or philosophy, or program, and just stick with that one person. When you're really excited about something, you want to find the answers. You want all the answers really quickly. You just want it right now.

So let me tell you that the most efficient way to get it now is to just do one thing at a time. Take one step at a time and have one person teach you their process. Make sure you resonate with that person or training and do your research. Don't be quick to jump into the newest shiny training or coach. Make sure you've really researched who you'll be working with, that you click with them, and that you like their integrity and who they are.

I remember a period when I was trying to do way too many things all at once. I was trying to get my website up, and trying to get my logo done, trying to get my first book done, and trying to re-do video webinars I had created, and trying to get everything ready for a launch. (The list is actually much longer but I don't want to bore you!) It was crazy! I was working with a bunch of different experts who all had different priorities for me. Because I was doing so many things, I was overwhelmed and stressed out. I was not getting anything done with any of them because I was too overwhelmed with all of them.

"Don't let yourself get yanked in all directions"

Don't let yourself get yanked in all directions. Focus on one step at a time and do a good job on it before moving to the next. As one of my coaches, Russell Brunson says over and over "Just One Thing!" And, boy, is he right. Once I understood the importance of focusing on one thing, I started to be much more efficient. It takes being disciplined. Even when you're working on just one aspect of your business, the other things haven't disappeared. They will still need your attention at some point. But if you try to do all of them at once, not only will you go crazy, but nothing will get done well or on time.

Focusing on one thing becomes part of your business planning. You've determined all the steps you need to take (at least, all the steps you know at this point) and the order in which you need to do them. Be clear on what you're going to do first. Down the road, you can always change your business plan if you learn something new. But changing your plan every three days or two weeks will keep you swimming in circles.

If you're going to hire a coach, don't get distracted by other coaches or do any other training. Do one thing at a time, see it all the way through. Implement what they recommend and give it time.

Enjoy the Journey

One lesson I learned is to enjoy the journey. It's something I've been really working on for myself: just being present in the moment. Many people who have an entrepreneurial mindset are constantly looking to the future. Once they get to where they want to go, they always want more and to take it to the next level. They're never satisfied and forget to appreciate where they've gotten and what they've accomplished. If you have an entrepreneurial type of spirit, you never really want to stop. You don't really want to retire because you enjoy what you're doing. There's nothing wrong with this at all. But I want to encourage you to try to appreciate each moment.

Enjoy the ride along the way. Understand that, hey, everything you're going through is happening because of the choices you have made, and everything is meant to happen. In doing so, it's going to help you learn and expand to the next phase. If you don't stop to enjoy what you're going through and what you're experiencing, you put an overwhelming amount of pressure on yourself and that's not fun. Keep the journey as fun as you can. If you get stressed, and worried, and overwhelmed along the way, sit back and say, "Okay, now how do I get myself more grounded, and appreciate what I'm going through, and appreciate these struggles? I may not get the lesson today, but I know I'm going to learn from these challenges!"

"If you don't stop to enjoy what you're going through and what you're experiencing, you put an overwhelming amount of pressure on yourself and that's not fun"

Celebrate your wins, even the smallest ones. Notice what you are accomplishing, and how much you are doing, and how far you have come. Write those things down. "Hey, today my win was X. Today, I accomplished X." Then, on days when you feel like you're going nowhere, you can look back and remember, "Oh, I did get that done this week! I got all these things done!" Understand success replicates success. So you need to be mindful of all of your mini successes so that you can continue to have more of them. This is far more important than you know. Recognizing what is working and noticing it will get you more of it, so take note and be appreciative of what you're accomplishing. For example, just as I am writing this, about five minutes prior, I gave myself a pat on the back for getting as far as I have. In fact, because I was giving myself kudos in recognition of how far I've gotten, it actually got me excited to want to continue to write more. And, that burst of energy all came from giving myself praises and recognizing what I've accomplished. Try it for yourself. Don't be so hard on yourself all the time. It's counterproductive.

"Recognizing what is working and noticing it will get you more of it, so take note and be appreciative of what you're accomplishing"

The Myth of the Overnight Success

You'll get there. It's just not going to happen overnight. That's another thing I learned along the way. Those "overnight successes" you hear about? If you really talk to them, they'll tell you about all the months they spent, all the mistakes they made, all the wrong turns they took. Then one day, all of those things came together to give them "instant" success! Trust me, "put up a website" or to create "a proto-type" is not a one-step process!

It really is a progression. If you want to change up your life and create something new that you love and can also monetize, it doesn't happen overnight. If you think it's going to, just stop right now. It's not going to happen, even for someone like me, who pushes, and pushes, and never stops, and has enough resources to hire help. It's still taken me sixteen months longer than I wanted to launch my business. Part of that is because I did it in the wrong order and should have just started on a smaller scale. Even with that being said, it just takes time.

> "If you're unhappy with what you're doing now, you're going to be unhappy in one year, in three years, in five years, in 10 years. You'll be unhappy until you finally make the conscious decision to do something about it and do whatever it takes to change it"

And we all have time, right? We're not going anywhere! You can either spend that time doing what you're doing and not enjoying it, or you can spend that time working on creating something you'll love. If you're unhappy with what you're doing now, you're going to be unhappy in one year, in three years, in five years, in 10 years. You'll be unhappy until you finally make the conscious decision to do something about it and do whatever it takes to change it. It might be a struggle. It might (truthfully, *will*) be a little bit harder than you thought. Success isn't going to be as quick as you hoped. But at least you won't be stuck regretting that you never tried.

Starve the Distraction

There's just so much noise out there all the time! What's really helped me focus is, first of all, making sure that I know exactly what I need to get done in a day, in each week, and each month. You need to stop long enough to figure out the main thing you want to accomplish each month. What's the biggest, most important thing? What's your priority for the month? And how are you going to take actionable steps toward that priority goal every single day?

Let's say that this month you want to start a Facebook group, and your goal is to have a thousand followers in it by the end of the month. That might be your macro goal, the most important thing for the month. Next, you need to say, "Okay, now, what can I do each week toward that goal so, at the end of the week, I know that I've made progress? What am I going to do each day?"

A big part of what happens when you're beginning is that you do get so overwhelmed by everything that needs to get done. And especially when you are putting the basics in place, you feel like you aren't getting *anything* done! You don't realize that you're putting critical building blocks in place. By knowing your macro goal, you can see how the steps are getting you closer to it.

Be clear about what you want to get done for each day. What works really well for me is to write it all down. At night before I go to bed, I write down everything that I want to accomplish that next day. I write down the top three things that I'd love to get done, then the one thing that, no matter what, I *have* to get done that day, so I can feel accomplished. You can write two or three, but what's the one major thing? By doing this, if you do at least one thing each day, and check off those little boxes, you're able to see what you're accomplishing. You realize you did get more done that you realized. It also keeps you on-track to make sure that you're actually doing what you need to do.

> "Be clear about what you want to get done for each day"

To organize your time, keep looking back at your business plan. Take stock of where you are in the plan and what your focus is supposed to be. Break down what needs to happen next based on where you are. Then look at the blocks of time you've committed to working on your business and schedule those tasks. One thing I can say is that, because we're all so busy, if you think it's going to take a week, it's probably going to take two. If you thought you could get it done in a day, don't beat yourself up for the times that you can't. Stuff happens. Don't make organizing your time and laying out goals a way to beat yourself up. Sometimes, you simply won't be able to accomplish things that you feel you should.

Pomodoro Technique

I ran across a technique that was developed in the 1980's and it helps with something most of us struggle with: time. If you're struggling with time right now, if you don't feel like you have enough of it, if you are feeling like there's just never enough hours in the day, if you're working yourself like a crazy person, try this out. It really works, and I've been using it more and more. You decide on one thing you're going to do. You set the timer for 25 minutes and really focus on that one thing. When the 25 minutes is up, you get up and walk around or stretch for 3-5 minutes. Then you set the timer for another 25 minutes and focus on that task again. When the timer goes off, you take another 3-5 minute break. Then repeat the process. After about four of these 25 minute sessions (they call them pomodoros), you take a 15 minute break. This is the break where maybe you can check your emails, respond to texts, clean the house, or just take a breather.

According to studies, you can get 16 hours more work done in a week by doing this. If anything comes into your mind during that 25 minutes, you write it down, but you don't do it. Though we've all got phones with timers on them, the guy who created this suggests using a mechanical timer. (The timer he originally used was a kitchen timer that was shaped like a tomato. Pomodoro is tomato in Italian!) He says the physical act of winding the timer is a physical signal that you're determined and ready to start that specific task. The ticking keeps you on track and the ringing signifies that you accomplished something and it's time for a break.

I turn off all notifications from my cell phone, Facebook, texts, *everything* while I'm doing this. And I totally screen all phone calls unapologetically. Just because the phone rings doesn't mean I have to answer it! I've read a bunch of research that says that trying to get something done with distractions is totally counter-productive. In a Careerbuilder.com survey, they found that distractions from cell phones are most common (52% of the 2,000 people said it was their top distraction), then comes the internet (44%), and social media (36%). A study from Oxford Economics says that general noise is another distraction. And another study showed that when you're distracted from what you're doing, it takes an average of *23 minutes* to get you back into really focusing on what you were doing again. I know this seems unreasonably long and inaccurate, but I've read a multitude of studies that agree with this, so heed the warning. If you're so busy you can't spare a moment, try using the Pomodoro Technique.

So that's where a lot of us are really losing time. Every time you go to check a voicemail, or go to send a text message, or go to check a "like" on Facebook, it takes you out of what you're doing. By being completely focused for just 25 minutes at a time, you can get an incredible amount accomplished.

For example, I might set up "Checking and Responding to Emails" as a 25minute task. Or I might set up "Researching X, Y, Z" as my task. Maybe it's working on a Power Point presentation or brainstorming ideas for content for your videos. It could be something that takes just one 25-minute period or something that will take several. The point is to do just that one thing for the entire 25 minutes without allowing any distractions.

Pay attention to the segments of your time rather than just floating through the day. If you don't use the Pomodoro Technique, you can still say, "Hey, I have one hour right now. I'm going to spend the next 60 minutes working on this specific activity. I'm not going to answer my phone. I'm not going to check my text messages. I'm turning all my notifications off, and not checking Facebook." That helps so much! During that hour as you think of other things that you need to do, you just write them down. But don't try to do them. Just stay focused on the specific task you started. You'll be amazed at what you can get done in a single hour just by staying laser-focused and not letting all the distractions pull you away.

"Pay attention to the segments of your time rather than just floating through the day"

TAKE ACTION #16

Test drive the Pomodoro Technique. Commit to using it as I've described for one whole week and notice if you become more efficient and productive when you use it.

Building Boundaries for the Clock

I've learned to schedule when I'll handle those distractions, like responding to phone calls, texts, and emails. My clients and staff know that I'll return phone calls between certain hours and respond to emails during certain hours. It's important to set expectations so you don't feel the pressure of someone freaking out because you didn't reply to their email or text within five minutes. If something is time sensitive or urgent, I've got someone on my staff assigned to respond. Every once in a while, it's something only I can handle but I try to make this the rare exception.

But by doing this, I'm being efficient and effective with my time, and serving my clients the best I can because I'm not being distracted. So, don't worry about it. Just decide, "I'm going to answer my phone at 9:00 in the morning, at noon, and maybe at 3:00, and at 6:00." Tell people to be clear about what they need so when you call them back, you'll be giving them what they need. Don't feel bad about this. It's setting proper expectations. If you set proper expectations with your clients, no matter what your business is, they're going to be okay with it and they're going to understand.

Another practice I encourage for time management is to get in the habit of audio books. When you drive to work or while you're getting dressed in the morning, listen to audio books that teach you something or inspire you. Rather than turning into the news or some talk show that has nothing to do with you, use this time productively to help you move forward.

Another thing that really helps me is making a note in my phone when I have a good idea. Often, good ideas come when you're in the middle of something else and you forget about them. Just jot them down in your notes section or even do a verbal recording. If you hear a good quote or something that inspires you, write it down in your notes. You may not have use for this quote or this idea right now. Just write things down so you can circle back to them later.

Growing Pains

Starting a new business or career means change. You might have to change your habits or how you spend your money. You'll have to do things you've never done before and learn things you didn't know before. You'll probably have to reach pretty far outside your comfort zone to create what you'd really love to have. It's a lot of change, and change can sometimes be very uncomfortable and just plain not fun.

When you're working toward a certain goal or you have something big you want to accomplish, it can take so much out of you that you feel like you want to stop. But you can't. Because if you keep on doing what you've always done, if you keep being the same person you've always been, you're not going to get a different result. You need to make some changes and be intentional about how you do everything.

And I know, it can hurt. It's like you just want to give up and not wake up in the mornings. Sometimes, you just want to sleep in, or you just want to eat that cheeseburger or have that glass of wine, or whatever it might be. It would have been really easy for me just to fall back into my comfort zone of just doing real estate. I'm amazing at it and totally comfortable in that arena. As I'm writing this book, I continue to do real estate part-time because I love it and I love serving my community. But I also feel like I've got a higher purpose, and I'm meant to teach, and I'm meant to coach, and I'm meant to inspire. In the beginning, I could have given up and gone back to real estate full time and just kept on being comfortable. If I'd done that, how would I feel five, ten years from now knowing I hadn't pursued that higher purpose?

One of my friends recently told me, "Krista, you're all over Facebook live and you're telling people about your stuff. Everyone knows everything about you now." It made me feel a little weird that she said that because it's true. I'm putting myself out there in ways I never did before. Sometimes during live sessions, I talk about things that are personal, things I didn't even have any intention of saying. I do it because I think it might help people I'm training and coaching. I also feel it's so important to talk about the hard things. Many people are only willing to reveal all of their successes. Think about how many times you've seen a couple posting about how in love they are, how wonderful every aspect of their life and family is, just to see them fighting a week later over who gets the cat in their divorce. My point is that people don't typically share their hard times with the world. We all have them. We work through them and hopefully are better for it in the end. So, if you're uncomfortable, often that's a good sign. If you're uncomfortable, and you're having a hard time with something, it means you're expanding and growing, so push through it!

"If you're uncomfortable, and you're having a hard time with something, it means you're expanding and growing, so push through it!"

Please remember, when you're trying to make a change and you're going through that discomfort zone, reach out to your support system. Reach out to your friends, reach out to a coach, reach out to a mentor. Find an accountability partner. Whatever it is that you might need to get you through what you need to get through. Do what it takes to get you to the next step and don't give up. To have a great something at the end, it's most likely going to hurt a little bit along the way. If you're telling yourself that every part of your life is okay and perfect, so you can coast from here on, remember, as soon as you stop learning, you stop growing.

I want to encourage you to embrace overwhelm when you feel overwhelmed. Stop and recognize how you're feeling. Then, instead of getting all frazzled and stressed, show appreciation for the overwhelm and remind yourself that you are feeling overwhelmed because you are learning, expanding and growing. It's a good thing, you're making change!

Manifesting Abundance

There is a huge difference between people who come from a mindset of scarcity and those that are focused on abundance. Honestly, I've had to go to counseling over this issue myself so I'm in no way an expert at this. I have my own worries about, "Oh my gosh! People are going to see what I'm doing and they're going to copy me and I'm going to lose business!" That's a scarcity mindset, like there isn't enough to go around so everybody can be successful. The idea that someone else can come along and steal my precious ideas so they'll win, and I'll lose. Your mind can go crazy thinking like that!

When your mind is really tuned into abundance, you don't freak out about competition. In fact, you almost welcome it. It makes you sharper and better at finding ways to be unique and improve. It helps you focus in on your own niche and specific market. You can share your ideas because you know you've got a million of them.

I coach some people who are in real estate to be better at what they are doing. At this point, I still have a real estate business, so they can be direct competition to me. Should I be worried that they're going to steal business from me when I help them get better? Maybe you're thinking, "Yes! You should be worried about that, Krista!" Guess what? I am not attracting the same clients that they are. There is so much business to go around that even if I could grab it all, I wouldn't be able to handle it. Real estate agents are taught to hoard every little bit of knowledge or good marketing ideas or potential leads because everyone is going to steal our stuff. Quite honestly, all someone would need to do is truly study my business and do their best to replicate it. (Though this would be tough to do because we do so much, and we continually modify, implement and evolve based upon new technologies and market trends.)

The scarcity mindset doesn't just happen in real estate. My friend Heather says that the mark of a real amateur in writing is when someone is afraid that their great idea for a book or screenplay will be stolen. She says, "Of course, you register what you've written. But the most important thing is to realize that a) you have many great ideas inside of you and b) there's nothing really new under the sun. Everything you come up with is just a variation on what someone has done before."

Anything that you're learning from this book or that my coaching clients learn is something I've learned from someone else. I didn't make it up. The information is out there, and anyone can go to all the trainings I've gone to and grab it. But nobody does. Or if they do, and they start training and coaching people, they still won't approach that coaching and training in the unique way I do. Clients that like my style will be attracted to me. Clients that like a different kind of style will go to someone else. There's plenty of business out there to go around.

So don't freak out if someone else is trying to copy what you do. Don't get all tight and fearful and worried about what someone else is doing. If they are infringing on your copyright or patent or pretending that some content you created is their own, yeah, you definitely want to call them on it. That's about integrity. But if they've just picked up some ideas or are mimicking your approach, forget about it. Just keep focused and moving forward in your business and continue to stand out and continue to provide real value. It will eventually pay off!

> "The more value you give your clients and customers, the more support you give others who are trying to be successful, then the more you'll receive yourself"

The more you give the more you get. Do we give because we want to receive? No, that's just the law of the universe, the law of attraction. It's pretty common knowledge that when you give you get more. The more value you give your clients and customers, the more support you give others who are trying to be successful, then the more you'll receive yourself.

I will tell you that I wish I had figured this out sooner. Even though I read a million books about abundance mentality versus scarcity mentality, my little brain did not seem to really get this until about six months ago. How sad is that for me? And since I've gotten rid of that scarcity mindset, my business has exploded.

Failure Breeds Success

I had a call recently with one of my former real estate coaching clients. She called me and said, "Krista, I'm having a nervous breakdown, I had this 2.5 million dollar listing but I ..." She went on for 20 minutes about how this great listing had fallen apart. She had literally been sitting in her room for two weeks, sad and depressed. Finally I said, "Just stop. Quit focusing on that. You've talked to me for 20 minutes and it's all 'poor me.' Things like that have happened to me. It's happened to everyone I know, and it's going to happen again. It's called business. Stop focusing on that and move on to the next. Figure out how you can help that next person and improve your business. Quit focusing on what didn't happen."

When things don't go your way, there are two things that you can do: You can be completely upset and ruin your day/week/month/life, or you can just roll with it and move on and make the choice to have a better outcome. We all go through challenges in life, whether it's personal, with your kids, your marriage, or your business. We all land in the muck at some point or another. It's how you deal with the muck that determines your outcome, not the muck itself.

> "It's how you deal with the muck that determines your outcome, not the muck itself"

Sometimes you look at other people and you just think that it's always been so easy for them. But I can guarantee you, it hasn't. Sure, some people get a break or two, but to stay on top, they worked at it too, tweaking and changing and doing everything they could to get where they are now. When you look at someone and they seem like they're just killing it, just remember that it took work, perseverance, consistency, and never giving up. You can be that someone too! Make the choice and just do it!

You may see someone doing really well in their profession, in a certain sport, or in academics. They make it look so easy, but it probably didn't look that way when they started. For example, I'm in a mastermind group with people from all over the world who are just truly amazing. Everyone there is super successful in their platform. They're all master marketers, and it's almost like they can just sneeze and make money! Even though I'm doing really well, when I look at them all, I think, "Wow!" Even though I've had amazing success in my real estate business and my coaching and training business is going gangbusters, these people are mega stars in what they are doing. Getting to their level takes time. So be willing to put in the time if that's your goal.

What do you do when you're expecting a certain outcome, and that outcome doesn't happen? How do you handle it? Do you wilt and whine, pull the covers up over your head and give up? Choose to fight back and push forward.

Your mindset is everything! Understand, you don't want to just start working on your mindset when everything hits the fan. Like a muscle, you want to build it up so that when you really need to lift that huge box or run that race, you're already in shape to do it. There are many ways to build up your mindset.

One of the things that I find helpful is getting up every single day and writing down all the things that I'm thankful for. Write down all the things that you're grateful for like good health, children, husband, relationship, friends, energy, all the things that you appreciate in your life. You'll get more of what you show gratitude for.

> "You'll get more of what you show gratitude for"

Another way to help with your mindset is by paying it forward as much as possible to other people. I watched a movie called *Pay It Forward* about 10-15 years ago. It was about this kid who ended up starting a movement where he would do something nice for somebody. Instead of wanting anything in return, he would tell that person, "Hey, can you do me a favor? Just pay it forward. Do something nice for somebody else." The idea of paying it forward spread like wildfire across the country with people doing random acts of kindness to pay it forward.

I've learned that the nicer and kinder you are to people, the more that you give and the more that you pay it forward, the happier you are and the stronger and more positive your mindset is. If you are having mindset issues, if you're struggling with your negative thoughts or discouragement, one of the best ways to combat that is by positively impacting the life of somebody else.

If you can get your mindset right, you can get anything right. If you can believe that you can do something, you can do anything. You cannot keep feeding your limiting beliefs if you want to succeed. You have to delete limiting beliefs every time they pop into your mind. Sometimes getting rid of negative thoughts is tough, especially with all the negativity we see on social media, on our phones, on the news. Everywhere you look, all you see is negative, negative, negative! You get what you focus on. So focus on what you can do and what you are good at, not what you can't do and what you're lousy at. Henry Ford once said, "Whether you think you can, or you think you can't—you're right." You can choose what you believe so why not choose to believe you *are* successful?

> "If you can get your mindset right, you can get anything right"

You have a choice to either allow all the B.S. to continue to run through your head and join the negative people around you. Or you can choose to be a ray of light and sunshine for those around you. The more that you're a ray of light to those around you, the more that you're going be a ray of light and positivity to yourself.

When you hit a hard time, try making life better for others. It doesn't have to involve money. It could be offering your time, giving someone a smile or a nice compliment, or going out of your way to help someone who is also having a hard time. When you do this, like magic, your own day gets better.

The Harshest Critic

This one is a big issue for most of us. We don't believe in ourselves enough. We have things we're worried about in life. We have hesitations. We're afraid to put ourselves out there. We're afraid to be different. We're afraid to go for it. We're afraid we'll fail. All because of our own self-limiting beliefs. These beliefs aren't the truth of who we really are, but we act as if they are. "I'm not smart enough. I'm not strong enough. I'm not talented enough. I don't have what it takes." And on and on.

A client of mine is a rock star. She's beautiful, not only on the outside but also on the inside. If you look at her, you would just think that she has it all going. Yet, it's so crazy to hear how much she struggles with all of her self-limiting beliefs and doubts. She was afraid to show the world her beauty and I couldn't believe it. I was just thinking, "What are you talking about? You're amazing. You're gracious. You're kind. You're smart. You have good intentions." But for quite a while, she couldn't get past her own limiting beliefs and issues.

We all have issues. We've all gone through stuff. We've all had bad things happen in our life that held us back and prevented us from moving forward like this client. The question is, how long are you going to stay stuck there? Get outside of yourself. Quit being so concerned with who you are or what people think about you and just put yourself out in the world. The day my client finally did that, I was so proud of her. It made me feel so good to know that she was finally going for it. You can continue to be a victim of your past or of your old story, or you can choose to make a new one, a story of victory and success. It's your choice. No more "poor me." Get over yourself!

> "You can continue to be a victim of your past or of your old story, or you can choose to make a new one, a story of victory and success. It's your choice"

I truly believe we all create our own destiny and our own reality. Have you ever known people who seem to constantly have bad stuff happen to them? They buy a car and it's a lemon. They go to a restaurant and the food is lousy (even though everyone else at the table had a great meal). They get passed over for promotions, store clerks are rude to them, and their iguana is always sick! And hopefully you know people who are the reverse, people who attract wonderful things to them. It has everything to do with your thoughts and mindset.

I highly encourage my clients to replace any negative thought with a positive one as soon as it pops into their head. Anytime a negative thought pops up (even if it sounds very true to you at the time), replace it with a good one. For example, if you think, "There is no way I'm going to get all this done today!" try replacing it with, "I have all the time I need" or "Everything will get done in its own right time." Or if you think, "That other person is way more talented than I am," try a thought like, "I have all the talent I need and am as good as anyone out there." If you practice this, pretty soon it gets easier and easier and you just see more and more of the positive.

We are all similar. We all go through struggles, problems, challenges. We all have the self-created obstacles that everyone else has. It's a matter how we handle them. Maybe you've had trauma in your life and you wake up in the morning and you're so very anxious and you have that horrible feeling in the pit of your stomach. You can't breathe and it's like you're having a heart attack. I had felt that way for as long as I can remember. Prior to doing EMDR with a counselor, I couldn't ever remember not feeling that way. I know I'm not alone in this. My conversation with one of my students the other night was:

"Hey, what you're feeling right now is not you now. It's not your true self. That feeling comes from another time in your life that you're holding onto. In the present, in this moment, you're a badass. You're a leader. You put yourself out there. You're doing what you need to do to move your life forward. You're being a world-changer. That's you now."

In most cases the feelings of inadequacy you have are from a different time in your life. If you can learn to identify what makes you feel inadequate or not good enough and the times in your life where those feelings first started, you can learn to overcome them.

For example, I suffered some very significant trauma when I was younger. So many times my feelings of anxiousness and anxiety as an adult stemmed from the anxiousness and anxiety I had as a child. Those feelings of being scared and nervous stayed with me for years and years until I identified that those feelings were from when I was a child. Now when I get nervous or anxious, I remind myself that those feelings of anxiety are not who I am today, but feelings from when I was younger. I remind myself that now I am strong, successful and safe and my anxiety ceases. I just have to be conscious of where those feelings truly are coming from and remind myself of what my current situation is so that my feelings are current. Make sense?

Next time you run into feeling rotten about yourself, try these tips:

1. Do a random act of kindness every single day for somebody not because we want something in return, just to help.

2. Focus on the positive about you and who you are. Focus on what you can become, what you can achieve, and the greatness you can be. Don't focus on the things that aren't who you really are. Make a list and focus on all the good things.

3. Love yourself and celebrate your successes. Continue breathing and learning to love yourself and appreciate all your experiences that made you who you are today.

Eye on the Prize: Be Unwavering!

Another key to dealing with setbacks and challenges is to keep your eye on that prize. If you begin to feel fuzzy or unmotivated, go back to your why and the vision you created. Why do you want this? Why is it so important to you? What is your end result? When you start feeling overwhelmed or burdened, you might feel like you want to give up. Hey, we all do at some time! But just remind yourself of the whole reason you're doing this new career or business in the first place. Remind yourself of how your life will change if you do push forward. Then remind yourself of what's going to happen if you *don't* do this. What result will you get if you give up? Remember, research shows that people's biggest regrets in life come from things they didn't change that they know they still can but choose not to.

"If you begin to feel fuzzy or unmotivated, go back to your why and the vision you created"

Accountability Buddy

If I offered my entire training program for free, yes, people would sign up, but less than 2% of them would actually do it. You know why? Because they would have no stake, no investment in it. They wouldn't have accountability.

Most often, people who want to achieve something big in life need a coach. They need someone to guide them. When I ask people why they want coaching, the number one thing is that they need accountability. Oprah gets coached by Tony Robbins. Tony once said to her, "Oprah, you're one of the most powerful, richest women in the world. Why are you coaching with me?" She said, "I need accountability." Why the heck does Oprah need accountability? She's a gazillion-air!

But Oprah is also very smart, and she knows that we all need to be held accountable. We need help. We need support. We're all human. As I'm writing this book, I just hired a leadership coach. Why? Because I'm now getting into the leadership role and I know this is not my strong suit and I want it to be. I'm also looking for a business-scaling coach because my coaching business is growing and expanding at a very fast pace, and I want to make sure my clients still get excellent service. And as I exit my real estate practice, I need to ensure it is set up to be self-sufficient when I am not present. I need to be a better leader. I need to have accountability that I'm actually implementing all the things I'm learning and teaching to others.

"As an entrepreneur, everything you do, wherever you show up, anything you put your name on is a reflection of who you are, what you do, and how you operate your business"

If you don't have a lot of money and you can't hire a coach, maybe you can find an accountability partner, or you can join a certain group of like-minded entrepreneurial people to support you in getting where you want to go faster. They can give you feedback, different ideas and a different perspective on what you're doing. You can share and learn from one another's experiences.

Live Your Brand

As an entrepreneur, everything you do, wherever you show up, anything you put your name on is a reflection of who you are, what you do, and how you operate your business. People pick up clues about who you are and what you're about through every little thing you put out there: your business card, your response to their questions, your blogs, the packaging you send your product in, your social media platforms and videos—everything!

It's as if you're constantly in a job interview. People will see how you run your business and how different (or not) it is from other businesses. When you meet them in person, they'll notice how sincere (or not) you are about their concerns. When you deliver your class, or training, or product or eBook, they'll pay attention to how much effort you put in (or not) and how much value you give them (or not). They can sense if you're just in it to make a quick buck or that you are truly trying to give them value. People can tell!!

So just like in a job interview, you need to put your best foot forward in everything you do. This doesn't mean you have to be perfect. People actually prefer that you're human and relate better to someone who is real. But it does mean that you need to give them at least 100%.

CHAPTER 8

Engagement Marketing

The next few chapters will be all about marketing and what you need to do to get yourself and your business out there. This is the area where most new entrepreneurs fall short. They just don't realize how much it takes to start getting those orders or new clients coming in. With as much experience as I've got in marketing for my real estate business, I'll be honest, even I didn't realize how much time and effort it would take to get my coaching and training business off the ground.

If you have no marketing experience at all, in a sense that's good. You won't be stuck in the mindset of trying to "sell" people on your product or services. Throwing out a bunch of "Hey, I'm great! Or "Hey, my product is great!" advertisements is the most ineffective way to market. The real heavy hitters in business—everyone from Ikea to Whole Foods—use an approach called "content marketing" or what I like to call "engagement marketing."

In engagement marketing, the idea is to create a relationship with your target market, so they come to know, trust and like you or your brand. How? By consistently providing them with something of value, information or insights or resources that can make their lives better or easier. Ikea has a website devoted to how to make your life less hectic. Whole Foods constantly gives tips on nutrition and health. They aren't touting their products but they're building a relationship with you, right? You can give your potential customers or clients this content in several ways (in blogs, emails, podcasts, videos, vlogging, articles) but the point is that you offer that value for *free.*

Okay, so you might be thinking, "How am I supposed to make money by giving away stuff for free?" I'm going to show you. But first get the idea in your head that you're going to give the people in your target market information they really want, and they can really use. You can only do that if you understand your client or customer avatar, your ideal client or customer, inside and out. What are their problems and issues? What do they want and need? (Later, we'll get into "Where do they pick up their information?" when we talk about platforms.) If you haven't done all the work to figure out your avatars, you'll have a hard time coming up with content or information that will attract them. If you have done that research and work, it's a piece of cake!

"When you give something to someone without asking for anything in return, it starts the law of reciprocity"

When you give something to someone without asking for anything in return, it starts the law of reciprocity. It's like when you go to the store and they give you a sample of a product. Many times you buy the product because you feel like you should since they gave you something. You often do this unconsciously. That's one reason businesses or non-profits send you a free pen in the mail, stamps, or address labels. It makes people feel like, "Oh, my gosh! I need to give something back." I even feel bad if I throw whatever it is away.

But keep in mind, unlike giving away cheapo pens, in engagement marketing, you're giving something that your avatar can really use. We don't use this "sales secret" to manipulate people but to truly be helpful to them. When they receive real value, they let their guard down. You're not being like everyone else pounding customers with just sell, sell, sell, take, take, take. You're give, give, give. So they feel more open to you and begin to trust who you are and what you have to offer. They can see that you're sincere about giving them value that applies to them. Not only that but it gives your client avatar a chance to see that what you have to produce is really great and you know what you're talking about. It gives you or your product credibility.

We'll talk about all the vehicles and platforms you can use for your engagement marketing in the next chapter. But for now, let's go through a bunch of examples so you get the idea of what engagement marketing looks like:

Take Modern Mom Lifestyle, the woman who offers everything from recipes to make-up tips for busy moms. She can research on LinkedIn and find professional women who are moms. Then she can email them and say, "Hey, here are five of my healthy crockpot recipes to save you time." She might then send a few other emails with tips like an article how to make a week's worth of healthy lunches or best foods to make ahead and freeze for later. After she has given them a bunch of valuable ideas for free, then she can say, "Hey, if you like my recipes and tips, you might want to buy my crockpot cookbook."

The woman who teaches boudoir photography can reach out to other photographers. She can say, "Hey, I just want to let you know I'm doing boudoir photography. Here are three of my best tips about how to make women feel more comfortable in that situation." Next, she could write a short article that says, "By specializing in boudoir photography, many people think it's bad for business. But I've found that having a niche has really helped me and here's why." She could then give them general tips like, "I found that by using a mirror and letting clients see themselves in the mirror, it takes less time editing. They can tell me up front what they like or don't like about themselves when they look in the mirror, then I can change the shots to accommodate them." She might send them one or two great tips every seven days or so. After a few of those, she might say, "Hey, if you're interested in learning a little bit on how to become your own boudoir, sign up for this free one-hour class." At the end of that free one-hour class, she sells them on her series of training videos.

Francel's company is called Back to Health Center, and her passion is training and coaching nurses on how to live healthier, more prosperous lives and be happier. So, she might begin her connection marketing campaign with an article on five tips for having a happier day at work for healthcare providers. She might send out a video that shows three techniques that will save their backs when they're lifting up patients. Her next email or Facebook post might be, "Hey, check out these three websites with great tips on X, Y, and Z" and one of them might be her own website with articles and tips and services she provides. Last, she might invite them to register for a course, sign up for her blog, join her private Facebook group and/or follow her on Instagram.

Let's say you're a bookkeeper who wants to create your own virtual bookkeeping business and your target audience is accountants who might hire you for projects. You could start by sending them tips on how to make tax season more efficient or how to pace themselves during tax season, so they don't get burned out. You could write an e-book that tells their clients how to best prepare the information needed to do their taxes. You could write an article that breaks down any new tax laws. And somewhere along the line, you could say, "Hey, is there any work that you'd like to farm out? I'm a bookkeeper."

Please notice that none of these examples was about sending out junk that isn't useful. The idea is to really think it through and send content that is specifically valuable to your avatars. You want them to start thinking, "Wow. He or she really understands who I am and what I need."

"You want them to start thinking, "Wow. He or she really understands who I am and what I need"

Think about the kind of things your audience is going through every day. When they see your videos or read your blogs, they are reminded that they feel the same things you feel. You're relatable to them. As you start to develop a following, they want to know more about you. Especially when you use video, people want to really get into your life. So, if you're not that person, and you're not comfortable with that, I wouldn't pick video as your vehicle. Blogging or even podcasts create a little more distance.

To find content and things to talk about, do some searches on Google. Google will show you what's trending and what's current. Think about your audience, what they need and want. How can you make their life easier? What value can you add to their lives? What can you give to them? What tips can help them succeed? And remember, when you're doing these videos or emails or blogs, don't ask for anything in return. You just give, give, give. And the more you give, the more that you'll end up receiving when you finally tell them about what you have to sell.

Get The Word Out With Your Story

As a marketer, you need to be a storyteller. Marketers are storytellers, and storytellers are marketers. Your goal is to include the Five E's in every video, blog or article: educate, entertain, excite, engage, and enthusiasm. Your free content should teach them something in a way that is fun, inspiring and relatable. Don't be intimidated by this! Think about when you tell a friend about some great hack you just figured out or some awesome deal you just found. As you're sharing it, you just have a natural enthusiasm, right? And you automatically try to explain it in a way they'll understand. That's all the Five E's are.

You want to capture their interest. You want to be exciting. Happiness sells. Excitement sells. Confidence sells. Also, at certain times, anger and anxiety sell. Happiness and excitement are about peoples' vision of the future. Anger and anxiety talks to their pain points. Now believe it or not, when you reach avatar's pain points and triggers, you also connect with them. The more confident you are about your product or service, the easier it will be to sell because they see that you believe in your own product or service yourself.

> "Happiness sells. Excitement sells"

One way of grabbing attention is creating a soap opera sequence. It can be a sequence of emails or blogs or videos. You start out with something dramatic and catchy and a title that makes someone really curious. For Natalie who has the Modern Mom Lifestyle site, her sequence began with, "The day I peed my pants on national television." For me, it was, "The day my family was ripped apart." For the boudoir photographer, it might be, "The day I realized my business could never go further."

In this beginning of the sequence, you start with your background, emphasizing problems or issues that people can relate to. Over the course of the soap opera sequence, you will tell your entire story about this problem and what you did about it. But the first email is just the beginning part of the story. You end each part of the story with something that will make them eager to read the next part that you'll send a couple of days later. You know those cliffhangers they use in television soap operas? "Oh, no! What is she going to do now that Gavin has discovered her secret?" Try to end each part of the sequence with something that leaves them wondering about what happens next.

This soap opera series could be an email or a video email. It could be a blog or a podcast. The point is to get people involved and intrigued so they want to find out what the next installment of your soap opera will be. You want to engage your audience and get them to want to come back for more. You also want them to realize you're not on a pedestal. Sometimes people see you as successful and they feel like you're different, maybe smarter or better than they are. They don't feel like they can accomplish or do what you've done because you have some super power or something. You need to help them understand that you are just like them. If someone like you, with all your problems and issues, can overcome those problems and issues, they can too. You're no different than they are.

To see an example of how this is done, go to: www.KristaMashore.com/soap-opera-sequence

In your soap opera sequence, tell them about some really hard times that you've gone through. Your message is, "I told you a story about myself. Do you realize that I'm just like you? And that I have struggles, and I've been at the very, very bottom. I lost everything, and I was able to rise up, and you can too." Of course, "being at the very bottom" might be the time when you realized that mice had taken over your house and all of the solutions you tried didn't get rid of them—until you discovered this awesome new solution which is your product!

If you're the kind of person who really needs to keep your distance, the soap opera sequence doesn't have to be about you. It could actually be about one of your customers or clients. You don't have to name names and you can change details to mask their identity. But by telling the story, you can engage your target market and get them to relate.

That said, I really urge you to be vulnerable in your blogs and emails and videos. Don't try to always be so perfect and so great. People resonate with you when you're vulnerable. They realize that you're just like them, that you have the same issues, that they're not alone. When you allow yourself to be vulnerable and talk about how hard it was to get to the top, the difficulties you're going through, and the pains you're having, your audience connects with you. They start to almost become a part of your family, your tribe.

"Don't try to always be so perfect and so great. People resonate with you when you're vulnerable"

Reel Em In!

When you offer something for free, you can use it as a lead magnet. You give people something and in return they give you their contact information, so you can stay in touch. But you can't ask for that information right up front. You've got to give, give, give first. Then after you've given them a ton of value, you take the next step and offer them something that they can get by clicking on a link. "Hey, I've got this free eBook on how to clean your car in less than twenty minutes. Check out this link." When they sign on that link, they actually have to put in their name and email address to see the clip.

Think of your marketing efforts like a funnel. You start by attracting a broad audience and you take them down a path. You continue to give them more of what they're interested in. Your audience starts to narrow as you offer more expensive or more specific services or products. That's okay because you end up with people who really want what you have to offer and will pay for it.

Again, don't ask for that information up front. Give things of value first. Then after you give things of value a couple times, create a lead magnet where they give you their contact information to get access to something like an eBook, pdf, video training or a webinar. When you have their email address, you can market to them in the future. BTW, asking for their phone number dramatically lowers how many people will respond. Initially you just want to ask for their name and email. Later on once you've developed more trust and credibility, it's okay to ask for this. But you don't need their phone number unless you are calling to sell them something or unless you want to text.

Video: Your Secret Weapon

Video is hands down the most effective way to do engagement marketing. Even if you are a little bit shy, I encourage you to try it. Something I always say is, "Be seen, be heard, be known." People need to know you in order for you to make an impact. You need to think of yourself as a product. If you're not selling a product, you're really selling yourself. Your services, your talent, or your knowledge is your product. And even if you're selling a product, it's even more powerful if your personality is attached to it, like Ben & Jerry's ice cream or Kobe Bryant's shoes. Your job is to be an attention grabber so that you can stand out from all the noise.

"Be seen, be heard, be known"

According to research, 87% of online marketers use video in their digital marketing strategies. Marketers who use video grew 50% faster in revenue than those who didn't. On social media sites like on Instagram, videos get 1,200% more shares than posts with just texts or photos.

Viewers retain 95% of a message when they watch it in a video, compared to only 10% when they read it in text. When people go online, they spend one third of their total online time watching videos. Also, 64% of customers say they're more likely to buy a product online after watching a video about it.

Video is the number one best thing that anyone can do to jumpstart their business. The number one thing in any business, no matter what it is, is video. Why? Because especially if you are your product (as in coaching or training or teaching or information), your job is to get people to know you, like you and trust you. Your job is to break down the barriers, that sense of lack of trust or belief people have. Videos are the fastest, most effective way to do this. Product videos help people make purchasing decisions for products. If you're the product, they need to see a video of you.

People are often concerned that it takes too much time to create a video, but it is really the fastest way to get your market to know and trust you (and in the next chapter, I'll show you how to get lots of mileage out of each single video by "repurposing" it). With all of the noise and stuff out there, people are afraid and don't know really who they can trust or who they can believe in. The more you use video, so your audience gets to see you, the more that you become a real person to them. They start to feel they know you because they see you so often on your videos. Once you start doing it and get familiar with making videos, it takes hardly any time at all. I can create a video now in less time than it takes to write an email or make a phone call!

To make it easier to record your videos, you can set a day aside each week where you record maybe eight content videos for the month, or four videos for the next two weeks. Schedule a specific time slot when you won't get interrupted. Get the room set up and be all ready to go with ideas of what you're going to say. Then for each video, just change your clothes and maybe change your hairstyle so you look a little different. Recording multiple videos at one time is much less overwhelming.

With videos, shorter is better. Keep them under 30 seconds if you can and give as much value as possible within that timeframe. Don't start by saying your name or introducing yourself. Start it with something really catchy. You have only 6 seconds to capture their attention so don't waste that time by saying your name. Make it count and hook them in immediately. For example, the Modern Mom might say, "Oh my gosh, I've got three huge tips that are going to save you so much time today." The photography person might say, "I just learned this amazing trick that just landed me five new clients." After the catchy opening, you can say your name.

A few years ago, people said that a three-minute video was good. All the research now shows 30 seconds or less is better. By the time this book is written, it might change again. A study I just read said that one minute of video is equivalent to 1.8 million words (which kinda makes me wonder why I'm writing this book!). Studies show that 20% of people will leave after the first 10 seconds of watching a video. So you need to make sure that you're engaging and motivating them to continue watching.

"Video mirroring" means emulating somebody else's video style that is working. Find someone who is doing something similar to you who is already well known and attracting followers. Watch their videos and webinars. Read their content. We call it "emulating." Follow somebody else who is doing well, see what they're doing, see what's working for them, and create a file and label it with their name. Then sit down with all the information you get from them and start studying them. Notice what's working for them. If it's working for them, it can work from you.

> "Follow in the footsteps of those who have figured it out then add your own personality, approach and knowledge to it"

When you watch someone else's video, you can even have that video transcribed. Learn the language of your successful competitors. Listen to the questions, feedback, and remarks that they're getting from their followers. Literally, make your competitors your personal mentors. Don't reinvent the wheel. I'm not saying to copy their material literally. That wouldn't be ethical. But learn from them then create your own material. Follow in the footsteps of those who have figured it out then add your own personality, approach and knowledge to it.

One of the biggest hurdles people have is the fear of doing video. They worry about having just the right equipment and set up. I tell people who are starting out that you just need to do it. In the very beginning, I would encourage you to set a goal and create a video every day. Send it to your friend, or send it to your mom, or send it to your spouse. Just ask them to watch it and critique you. No one is perfect, and no one expects you to be perfect. If you don't just start, you never will. You've just got to put one foot in front of the other and do it.

Don't worry about the lighting or getting a tripod or how your make-up looks or having the perfect backdrop. All of those are just excuses, right? Everybody has a cell phone. Right now, just use your cell phone. Pick it up, push record, make sure you've got decent light, and go for it. Your goal with these first videos is to just get comfortable doing it. No one will see them (except your mom). By watching your own videos, you'll see what you need to improve on. Whenever you do a video, record for a few seconds then check it out. Make sure the lighting is okay, so you don't have some crazy glare. Make sure you can actually see yourself. (Yes, I've recorded a whole video where the camera was off or my phone was filming my feet!) Make sure that the background is appropriate (I made a video at home once then discovered my undies were drying in the background!) and that you can hear yourself clearly (no dogs barking or wind howling). If everything checks out, just go ahead and record your video. You can do a couple of takes but do NOT try to be perfect! Imperfect is much more engaging and relatable. Remember, it's okay to be perfectly imperfect. Just start and do it!

TAKE ACTION #17

Take out your cell phone right now and make a quick video about your product or service. Pretend you're talking to a good friend or your mom. Just answer the question, "Why would someone be interested in what you offer?" Don't make a big deal of this. Just do it! See? Easier than you thought, right?

Now go to Facebook and sign up for the group on Facebook called________________________. Post your first video and ask for constructive criticism from the group. This group will be an excellent place for you to get help and work with fellow entrepreneurs who are in the exact same boat as you are. You can utilize this group to ask questions, help keep you accountable and, of course, to give as much value as you can to others. Again, the more you give, the more you'll receive.

So let's talk about some content that could be especially good for video. (Hey, wait, did you post your video into the Facebook group yet? If not, get over your fear, put this book down, and take your first step towards learning how to feel comfortable using video so that your audience can get to know you!) The woman who started the bridal boutique could record a video showing the different types of dresses that are flattering for different body types. She could do videos on how to buy a million-dollar dress on a hundred dollar budget. A fun video could be taking a dress that's really inexpensive and showing that you could just add this, this and this, now the dress looks expensive but, it isn't. She could do a video of the five top appetizers you can serve at a wedding for the least amount of money, or different items that you could use at a wedding to have your wedding pop. She could create a video series on theme weddings. So if you're trying to have a country wedding or you're trying to have a modern wedding, what kind of things should you have at each one?

She could create a video on who typically pays for what in a wedding. What is customary? She can do a video on different resources that you can utilize when you don't have the resources. She could come up with dozens of helpful videos. Then, of course, during the videos as she's giving good information, she's always somehow subtly promoting her own products and her own business.

What if you wanted to turn your knack for being a great party planner into a business? You could do videos on different decorating ideas and different decorating themes, decorating on a budget, or decorating when you have a lot of money. You could recommend places to go for certain types of things. "If you're going for a western theme, here are five resources for a western décor. If you want to do a Hawaiian theme, here's good Hawaiian resource." You could pick different themes and show people before and after of what it would look like using video or even just pictures. Then you can create an eBook or webinar to sell on how to make parties really fun and successful.

Or with that same party planning business, you could focus on newlyweds, or young people who haven't done a lot of entertaining. You could make videos that talk them through the whole process. "If you're going to have six people over for dinner, you want menus that are simple. Here's a fail-safe menu that you can put together." "If people coming to your house are drinkers, this is how much wine you might need." You could teach real basic information for somebody who's never entertained before, so they don't have to be nervous about having guests. Your business could be opening up your own entertainment store, or you having your own awesome YouTube or Facebook channel, or actually having your own television show. You just never know where it can lead.

> "The more you teach people, you give them value, and you're helping them and showing them that you're an expert, they're going to want to do business with you because they know you"

My husband is a car guy. He owns an auto body shop. I tell him, "Guys love seeing before and after." He could make little videos on ways to be more efficient when painting a car, or how to have a better paint job, or how to make your paint last longer, or when you should or shouldn't paint the car, or how different climates effect it. The more you teach people, you give them value, and you're helping them and showing them that you're an expert, they're going to want to do business with you because they know you. They know that you're knowledgeable, and know what you're doing. They know you're an expert without you telling them that you're an expert. It is implied. This approach works for any business and it doesn't matter whether you're brand new or if you've been in the business for ages.

What if you are a contractor? You could do videos on what homeowners should look for in a contract when hiring a contractor. You could talk about or even show the big mistakes people have made in remodeling. You could also talk about or show five of the best things you can do to improve a home. You could talk about ways to save money but still have an amazing house. You could show before and after videos of homes you've remodeled. You can even show yourself working on the project in fast motion. People love this stuff! By the time they've watched all your videos, prospective clients will feel like they've already met you, as if they know you.

What if you are just really good at errands and love to run around doing them? You could focus on the elderly (or people with elderly parents) with something like, "We'll do your errands for you. We'll pick up your groceries for you. We'll do the things that you can't do because you don't want to leave the house. We'll get you to your doctor's appointments. We can do all those kinds of things."

You can start as simply as doing little tips on Facebook. You could talk about what happens as you get older and advise people on things that they need to be cautious of. You can give five tips on how to ensure that your parents are safe when they're not around you, for example, making sure that you have a certain time every day that you talk to each other, and if you don't, you know there's an issue. Or you can tell them where they can get one of those emergency monitors for their parents. You could talk about ways to check out people who do work for their elderly parent to make sure they aren't taken advantage of and that they remain safe. Then, by you giving those tips, they're realizing that, "Wow, you really care!" Then they feel more comfortable having you actually care for their elderly people, or having your company care for them.

> TAKE ACTION #18
>
> Sit down and make a list of topics for videos, blogs or podcasts that would be good for what you have to offer. Remember, we're not selling here. We're giving value. We're educating, entertaining, exciting, engaging, and being enthusiastic. So think of a bunch of topics that would be of value to your potential customers and clients. What do they need? What would they like? What could make their lives better?
>
> Next, take each idea and break it down into just 3 to 5 tips or bits of information that are most important. In a short video, that's really all

you have time for. If you have more material than that, set your videos up as "part one" then "part two."

Video Tips & Tricks

I know people who have set up mini studios in their homes with backdrops, professional lighting and a regular video camera. If you want to do that, go for it! I do create professional quality videos for my training videos. But for engagement marketing, I just use my cell phone or my computer. It's more personal and it saves a lot of time on set up. And once you've done it a few times, you'll find that it's easy and you can do videos on the spur of the moment when a great topic hits you.

To create good videos on your cell phone, you'll need a Smartphone - iPhone/Android, a mobile device tripod, and a microphone for your mobile device, either a lav mic or a shotgun mic. The stability of the tripod gives your video a much better look. A lav mic does a good job of reducing wind and background noise so use one when possible. A shotgun mic is good for videos on the run. It still picks up great audio (though doesn't cancel as much background noise as a lav mic) and doesn't have to be attached by a cord to your phone. I recommend a BOYA BY-M1 for a lav mic and Rode VideoMic Me for a shotgun mic.

When you've got what you need, take these steps to get yourself ready to create your video:

1. Organize Your Content: Think about the main points you want to make and how you might make them. Get prepared with a snappy beginning like, "These tips will save you so much time today!" Most of your videos will be super short so try to do them without notes if you can. Approach it as if you are just telling it all to a good friend.

   If I have a longer video, I use an app called Prompt. However, most people look very unnatural on a teleprompter. You know your topic so just use bullet points to remind you of what you want to say. It's easier and often I find my videos turn out better when I am not overly-rehearsed.

2. Select a Suitable Location: This is important. The setting behind you should be aesthetically pleasing without taking away from the subject (you). Keep it simple and uncluttered. You also want minimal background noise so close doors and windows. Overly dark areas and overly bright areas should be avoided also.

3. Set Up Good Lighting: Natural light is your best friend in creating a professional looking video. But of course, it's not always available. Be sure to *face* whatever lighting you have. Never shoot with natural light or other

lighting behind you. Either face it or have it shine at you from the side (balancing the opposite side with another light source). Use what you have! You can light yourself up with a freestanding light, a desk lamp, or any light source that will light up the shadows. If you want to invest a little more, feel free to use lighting kit gear. But a great looking video can be achieved with what you have around you.

4. Set up your Tripod: Setting your cell phone at the right height is a simple but important way to make your video look more professional. Set up your tripod just below eye level whether you are sitting or standing. You want to be looking slightly down at the camera on your phone. A height-adjustable tripod is ideal. But you can also use the things you have around you to get the right height (stack of books, tables, chairs, etc.) If you can't set up your tripod, another way to stabilize your video is to use a selfie stick.

5. Mount Your Phone on the Tripod: You want to make sure you mount your phone *horizontally* (landscape) for the best look and be sure to use the front facing camera so you can see the screen as you record. Clean the camera on your phone as it can become smudged from storing it in your pocket or purse.

Check that you have enough free space on your phone to record a video. If not, backup your files onto your computer and delete them off your phone. Also, turn your phone onto airplane mode so that notifications, texts and phone calls don't interrupt your recording.

6. Set Your Phone Exposure to Manual: Your phone adjusts from light to dark in a video recording to adjust to all the high and lows of light in any situation. To avoid this happening while filming, turn on AE lock on your iPhone. Tap and hold on the camera screen for the area you want to expose (which should be yourself) and hold it down until you see "AE Lock" (auto exposure lock). Adjust to the exposure you want by sliding your finger up and down. Android users may have to download an app to adjust and lock your exposure manually (such as the app Open Camera in the Play Store). There is a lock symbol with a plus and minus sign to adjust and lock the exposure you want.

7. Wire Up Your Microphone: Plug the mic jack into your phone and clip the microphone onto your shirt or jacket. Make sure it isn't positioned near jewelry or anything that it could hit as you move. If you do not have a lav mic, sit close to your phone in a quiet setting. Open up your camera to your front facing view and switch to video mode.

8. Frame Your Shot: Make sure the shot is level, noting if any lines behind you or anything on the horizon look crooked. It's best to not be front and center in your shot. You want to be slightly off to the side and looking across the camera into the camera lens. Always look directly into the camera lens and

not at yourself on the screen. By doing so, you'll have direct eye contact with your audience.

9. Record a Quick Test Run: Record just a few seconds and play it back to check lighting, sound quality, background, angles, if you're looking in the camera correctly, etc. Make adjustments and do another quick test prior to filming the entire video. I can't tell you how many times I've recorded with no sound or while the camera was pointed at my feet!

10. Record Your Video: Get in position, hit record and pause for 3 to 4 seconds smiling at the camera. That way, you'll be able to edit out the part where you reach over and turn the camera on so the first thing they see is your smiling face. Remember to look in the camera, not your image on the screen. If you have sudden background noise or disturbance, pause and re-start your sentence so nothing is lost. When you finish, pause and smile for 3 to 4 seconds again.

Here are a few more tips to help you look better on camera:

- There is nothing more uncomfortable than watching someone who is uncomfortable on camera. Your viewers and audience want you to look relaxed, so they can relax and enjoy your content. Remember, it's okay to be perfectly imperfect. It's okay to make mistakes. You are not a robot and people won't relate to you as much if you are. So get out of your own head and just do it. You'll get better and better over time.

- Remember to smile and blink. When we physically smile, it actually creates a natural reaction in our minds to relax and breathe which ultimately makes you look more comfortable and confident on camera.

- Playback your videos and watch yourself. Notice things you like and work on the things that you don't like. But do not shame yourself or feel embarrassed. It's not natural for any of us to talk to a camera.

- Posture is important. Chin up and shoulders back.

- Be yourself. There's a reason that people in your life who already like you, like you. Odds are, your audience will too.

With anything in life, the more you practice the more comfortable you'll be. Keep your first videos simple so you don't get overwhelmed. Once you feel more confident, you can start adding music and graphics, even animation. Check out royalty free music on YouTube's audio library (Click on YouTube profile picture in upper right then Creators Studio then Audio Library to find resources like epidemicsound.com, soundstripe.com, pond5.com, and freestockmusic.com). Remember that you only have 6 seconds (which is the attention span of a goldfish) to grab someone's attention. So you want your videos to pop visually. You can find plenty of great apps that are free or very inexpensive to assist with editing, animation and graphics (just be sure they are compatible with your device). For Android, check out VideoShow, PowerDirector Video Editor, KineMaster, Quik, VivaVideo, Funimate, Magisto Video Editor & Maker, and Movie Maker Filmmaker. For an iPhone, you can look into Videoshop, Splice, Cameo, Quik, Video Crop, and Magisto.

TAKE ACTION #19

Make your first content video. Use one of the topics you listed. Get what you need and follow the steps above to set yourself up. Don't make a big deal about it! With a little practice, making videos will become like tying your shoe. And even if it takes a little effort and determination to get started, it will be SO worth it to your business. So just do it!

CHAPTER 9

Marketing in the Digital Age

In the beginning, I had hired a coach to help me start my new business. She trained us to build our contact list by doing something called a Summit. A Summit is when you interview professionals in the field of interest of your avatar. You interview them, and then broadcast the interviews to your clients or perspective clients to get them to want to join or give their email address in exchange for all of the Summit speaker interviews. The idea is also that the speakers have a huge list and will share your Summit with their list thus building up your own email list.

I have to say, this was a huge endeavor: interviewing, taping them, getting interviews edited, uploading, marketing for the Summit, creating email sequences and follow up campaigns—it went on and on and was very time intensive. I wasted over 4 months doing this with two full time helpers. We followed the protocol to the letter. The result? Just 1,110 new contacts. In comparison, I created a target market ad on Facebook and spent just above $300.00 and got over 1,300 email addresses and opt-ins in *one* weekend with *one* ad running. That is what I call 21st century marketing!

Okay, so you've come up with some good content and started making videos and writing blogs. Now what? How do you get that great content out to the people you want to reach? The most important rule of thumb is to show up where your target market is. If you were a huge company that advertised on TV, you would choose the shows that your target market watches, right? Your ads targeted to kids would show up on Nickelodeon but if your target is young men, you might go for ESPN. Then you'd refine it further by picking specific shows, for example, the Ellen Degeneres Show is a favorite among women who are 25 to 54.

> "The most important rule of thumb is to show up where your target market is"

No, I'm not recommending that you market your new business on television! Marketing through the internet is way more cost effective and with all the new technologies out there, you can get your message to thousands of your avatars almost instantly. But you still want to focus on using the correct platform(s) for the target market you've identified. It's really important that you pick a platform wisely, then master that platform and do it relentlessly. You want people to get familiar with you and count on your showing up on that platform before you expand to other platforms. If you try to do all of them or even a few of them, you won't be effective on any of them.

> "It's really important that you pick a platform wisely, then master that platform and do it relentlessly"

Pick one and master it and then move on to another one. This way you can learn what works and what doesn't and you're not wasting money on all platforms in order to figure out what works. You may be able to save time and money once you start marketing on another platform based upon what you learned from the first. Unless you have unlimited time and resources, I'd suggest starting on one.

Every platform works differently and has different tools to use. I'd really recommend taking a class or tutorial on any platform you decide to use. Too many people are on a platform but really have no idea of all the things it is capable of doing. Don't be that person. Find out all you can about the platform you plan to use.

Choosing Your Platform

So how do you pick your platform? Fortunately, studies can give you all the statistics you'll need to figure out which internet platform your people go to most frequently. Here are some insights on some of the most popular:

Facebook:

I use Facebook extensively. I think of Facebook as a place to market personal services or products as opposed to business to business services. According to Zethoia, there are 2.3 billion active users on Facebook. The average person visits Facebook 17 times a day and spends 51 minutes on Facebook. Five new profiles are created every second on Facebook, and 76% of users are female. Here's the breakdown on the ages of Facebook users:

18-24 - 18%

25-34 - 26%,

35-44 - 19%

45-54 - 16%

55-64– 7%

65+ - 10%

The highest traffic happens mid-week, between one and three pm. On Thursdays and Fridays, engagement is 18% higher (meaning that people actually like or share or open posts).

You can create a Facebook page that is specifically for your new business. In fact, many people now do this instead of creating a traditional website, but you really should do both. You need a website because if something happens to Facebook, your audience is gone. If your Facebook page gets blocked or banned for a weird reason, you're out of luck. You don't own anything on Facebook. It's like renting a home: You can be evicted at any time, with or without reason.

You can post photos and videos and articles on your Facebook page and you can invite people to events. On a Facebook business page, you don't "friend" people, but you ask them to like and follow your page. Your business page will have information about your business and you also want to put some personal stuff on. Let yourself be vulnerable so people can relate to you. People are trying to get to know you, and the idea is to develop as much trust as possible as viewers look at your page.

Give as much value as you can on this page. With your target market in mind, create posts with helpful tips for them or videos that teach something they need to know. The more your avatar sees you, the more they recognize you as a trusted authority figure in your field. Give as much information, value and tips as you can so, eventually, they will want to buy what you offer because they trust you. It typically takes anywhere from eight to twelve times of exposure for people to even click or want to engage with you. So it's really important to be very consistent about this. Keep giving value. Keep creating and posting new things. This applies to other platforms as well.

Facebook also has Ad Manager, an incredibly useful tool. You can set up an Ad Manager account which you create through your Facebook business page. An Ad Manager account helps you do target marketing and even re-targeting. The Ad Manager account is free though you pay for each specific ad. Here's what's so incredible about using the Ad Manager account correctly. You create an Adwhich can have a multitude of objectives. From your ad, you can determine what you want the outcome to be. Right now, Facebook's objectives are reach, brand awareness, video views, traffic, lead generation, conversion, and engagement. You can choose for the ad you are running to have a specific objective, like a post, video, landing page, or lead generation ad, then you tell Facebook exactly who, what, when, and where to send it. Now granted, this is a very broad overview of how Facebook works. It is way more complicated, but you get the idea here. It would take an entire book or course to break down exactly how all of this works. In fact, Facebook has a multitude of objectives you can choose from.

Facebook basically is an algorithm and Facebook wants the user, which is everybody on Facebook, to enjoy their experience. So, Facebook tracks what people are searching, what their interests are, the things they like, what they comment on, and what they do. With that information, Facebook is able to send them more of the stuff they might like. Facebook wants our marketing to work because the more our marketing works, the more that we target our right audience, the more money Facebook makes.

When you go into your Ad Manager account, you can set up a target market based on your understanding of your perfect avatar. You can specify age, gender, income level, interests, hobbies, and careers of your target market. You can specify hundreds and hundreds of different behaviors like people who work in real estate offices or people who like Tony Robbins or people who watch *Ellen*. There are hundreds of different things that you can target market in Facebook. Through Ad manager, you can include certain people or exclude certain people. For example, if you are a personal trainer and you have a really clever promotion you want to run, you may want to exclude other personal trainers, so they don't steal your idea right away.

You can specify people within a 60-mile radius of your location or people with an interest in photography or even specifically, women who have an interest in photography. It's very detailed and specific so you can direct everything to your best target market. You can only do all of this through your business page on Facebook and Ad Manager, not your personal page.

You can also be super specific as to the result you're trying to get. For example, you might want to create an ad that gets lots of video views or one that reaches the masses. If you say that your objective is to get lots of video views, Facebook will find people who like watching videos and it will push your ad to them. If your objective is to reach the masses, it will push it out to everyone. If your objective is to get people to engage by sharing, commenting or liking your post, Facebook will look for people who like to do that. You can also create a lead magnet ad designed to get people to give you their contact information.

You can set up an ad specifically designed to get likes on your business page. Likes are important because it gives you credibility and sets you up as an authority. When people go to your page, if they see you've got a lot of followers, a lot of likes, and a lot of members in your group, they see you as more legit.

You first have to create an ad using video or photos or whatever you've chosen. Then you go into your Ad Manager account and say, "OK, here's the ad I created and here's who I want to see it. I want this to be an engagement ad or I want this to be a video view ad or I want this ad to reach the masses." Facebook then distributes it according to what results you want.

The important thing about using an Ad Manager account is that you can create audiences then you can re-target to the audiences you create. For example, say you run an ad to get people to know you and you're targeting moms. You give away five of your best recipes for free. When you go into your Ad Manager account, you can see who clicked on your ad to get the recipes. These are people you want to re-target and give them things that are similar to what they originally were interested in. You can also see how many times your ad was viewed or how long your video was watched. You can then create a retargeting ad based upon the results you've gotten from the ads you've run.

Facebook uses the information about who you're trying to target and your results. So you can go to your account and say, "I want to create another audience. Anybody who clicked on my last ad, I want to re-target to those people." Your Ad Manager account can show you that certain people actually watched one of your videos about a cookbook. You re-target them with a cookbook ad. If others viewed your video ad on doing makeup, you re-target them with makeup ad or how to style your hair in 15 minutes. Each time you do this, you're zeroing in on people who will be active clients or customers.

Another great tool within your Facebook Ad Manager account is that you can create lookalike audiences. Once you create ads that work properly for you and you're reaching your target audience, you can create a lookalike audience, meaning, you tell Facebook to put your ad in front of people who have similar traits, likes, and interests as the people who have already interacted with your ads. This tool is just amazing and can help your marketing dollars go much further.

LinkedIn:

LinkedIn is a platform built for business professionals. It's not a place where you're going to find cat videos or a photo of someone's plate of lasagna! LinkedIn markets business to business and it's more of a professional platform. So, if you want to connect with and target accountants, doctors, lawyers, real estate agents, lenders, or any kind of a profession, you want to be on LinkedIn for sure.

As of January 2018, there were 500 million LinkedIn users worldwide and 133 million in the U.S. Forty percent of all LinkedIn users go to the site daily. Some other interesting facts:

44% of Linked users earn more than $75,000 in a year.

40 million students and recent college graduates are on LinkedIn.

28% of all male internet users are on LinkedIn, and 27% of all female internet users are LinkedIn.

After US, India, Brazil, Great Britain and Canada has the highest number of LinkedIn users.

13% of Millennials (15-34 Years old) use LinkedIn.

Two new users sign up every second!

LinkedIn now has 3 million active job listings on the platform.

59% of LinkedIn members have never worked at a company with more than 200 employees.

There are 5.5 million accountants on LinkedIn.

A lot of people use LinkedIn to find jobs or to fill jobs, but many homebased businesses use it as well. If LinkedIn is right for their business, the first thing I have clients do is set up a LinkedIn profile. The profile should reflect the business you are building, and it should be complete. Make sure you use a professionally-taken photo for it. And make sure you answer all the questions - interests, past jobs, etc.—because you never know what might connect with people when they're viewing your profile.

Next you start building your network. You reach out to professionals you know who are on LinkedIn and other businesses and request to connect with as many people as possible. You can also join industry or interest groups on LinkedIn to make more connections. Take the quick course LinkedIn offers online.

When you connect to a person or business, it'll show you who else they're connected to. Once you've made those connections, make sure you follow up. Wish people happy anniversary of their business and congratulate them for business wins or promotions. One great part of LinkedIn is that people can post testimonials about you and you can post testimonials for other people. This is a great way to build credibility and build trust with your connections. Give a testimonial if you can. Before you ever ask anybody for anything, be sure to give them something of value.

For example, let's say you're trying to reach chiropractors. You could give business tips or make an ebook on "five things to make a chiropractor office run more efficiently." You could do a short video on how to make new patients more comfortable or how to deal with problem employees. You want to give them four or five things before you ever ask for anything. For any group you're targeting, you need to think about how you can help the person that you're trying to attract. Before you ever ask for anything in return, how can you benefit their business or their lives? I would individually market to people, and send them a private email directly to give them something of value. It could be, "Hey, here's five tips that made my chiropractic business more successful," or "Here's three great reads," or "Here's a great accounting software that helped my chiropractic business."

You can also purchase ads on LinkedIn, so you can stay in front of the avatars you are trying to reach. It works just like Facebook ads, only different! Again, you need to study whichever platforms you choose to learn how to properly use their system to promote your product or service effectively.

Instagram:

Instagram has over 800 million Instagramers (up from 600 million in 2016). There are 500 million active users each day, and 51% of Instagramers say they access it on a daily basis (35% of users look at it several times per day). About 95 million photos and videos are shared on Instagram every day.

About 50% of Instagramers, follow at least one business. Instagram posts with hashtags will average 12.6% more engagement than those without. Posting at 5 pm on Wednesdays gets more engagement than any other time. Here is more information on people using Instagram:

Most users are between the ages of 18 to 29

Women are more likely to use Instagram than men, 38% versus 26%

32% of teenagers say that Instagram is an important social network

32% of Instagram users attended college

6 out of 10 online adults have Instagram accounts

26% of Instagram users make more than $75,000 per year.

25 million businesses have profiles on Instagram

2 million businesses run ads every month

Over 80% of accounts on Instagram follow a business

60% of users say that they have learned about a product or service on Instagram

The value of Instagram is that you draw people into your world so they get to know you. This is in turn builds trust and they are more likely to purchase from you. It's all about know, like and trust. Instagram lets you post stories, where you can show snippits of your day. It's almost getting more popular than just posting one picture or video because it's nice and quick. You can quickly see what someone's entire day was like by looking at their story and you get to see all about them very quickly.

In business you could show quick pictures of you, your product or service so people can get a quick glimpse of what you do. If we take Natalie as an example, she could take quick snapshots of her day to show to all her moms. This helps people relate to her and get to know her. She could take a photo of what she made her kids for breakfast with a note that it only took her 7 minutes to make it. She could do a quick before and after picture of getting ready, and give tips on how to get ready in minutes but still look like a million bucks.

Twitter:

Twitter has 330 million monthly active users in more than 40 languages. Only 69 million of those 330 million monthly active users are in the United States, so 79% are international users.

21 % of American adults use Twitter.

36% of Americans aged 18 to 29 years old use Twitter

22% of those aged 30 to 49 use Twitter

18 % of 50- to 64-year-olds

6% of those aged 65 and up

So Twitter is a younger crowd and Twitter itself says that 80% of its users are "affluent millennials." They also tend to be educated:

28% of Americans with a college degree use Twitter,

24% of those with some college education

14% of those with a high school diploma or less

And affluent:

35% of Americans who earn $75,000 or more use Twitter

26% of those who earn between $50,000 and $74,999

16% of people who earn between $30,000 and $49,999

18% of those who earn less than $30,000 per year

Twitter reports that the top reason people visit Twitter is to "discover something new and interesting." 93% of people who follow small- and medium-sized business on Twitter plan to purchase from the businesses they follow[4]. 69 % have already purchased from a business because of something they saw on the network. A third of users who follow a business have retweeted a business Tweet. 83% of people who Tweeted at a business and got a response, came away feeling better about that business.

A quarter of U.S. marketers run video ads on Twitter. Most Twitter users don't perceive video ads as intrusive[5]. In fact, most Twitter users found the video ads to be informative.

85% of Twitter users who follow medium-small businesses said they believe Promoted Accounts help them discover new businesses, and 68% have followed a business after seeing their Promoted Account.

A Nielsen study commissioned by Twitter found that a quarter of new vehicle purchasers in the U.S. said they used Twitter as part of their decision-making process when buying a new car. Twitter's own data shows that 41% of people on Twitter purchased products after exposure to an ad in the last 30 days.

You can use Twitter to promote your business in several ways:

1. Position yourself as a thought leader

by sharing imformation that is important to your target market.

2. Add value

. Remember to give, give, give rather than just selling yourself or your product. Retweet posts from people or businesses to develop relationships. Answers questions that people Tweet to you. Post things that your target market really cares about.

3. Follow first before engaging

. If your target market includes other businesses or professionals, follow their Tweets for a while to see how they engage and what's important to them.

4. Share your personality

. As with every other platform, sharing who you are helps people trust you. This doesn't mean you have to share everything about your personal life but let people see the human side of you.

5. Keep it relevant

.Your Tweets and what you retweet needs to be relevant to your target market. Retweets can be seen as endorsements so make sure whatever you retweet really fits with you, your brand, and your business. For the most part, you probably want to stay clear of political or controversial subjects.

6. Take the conversation elsewhere

. Twitter is a vehicle for making connections. Once you have established a connection, 140 characters is too limiting to take the relationship further. Instead, move to direct messaging, email or phone

YouTube:

YouTube is a little different than other platforms. You can actually have your own YouTube channel where you can upload your videos and people can find them. People search YouTube for just about anything and everything. YouTube is an information network. People are making money on YouTube like crazy. If you get a lot of followers, businesses will pay you to run their ads on your page. They will also pay you to promote their products as you get popular enough. So you'll want your information about your product or service to be on YouTube.

YouTube has over one billion users which is one third of the total internet users. About 300 hours of video uploaded every single minute on YouTube. Around 5 billion videos are watched every day and 30 million people visit YouTube per day. Eight out of ten YouTubers are between the ages of 18 and 49, and 6 out of 10 prefer video platforms over live TV.

The crazy thing is ALL of these platforms need their own book on how to work them. And by the time that book is written, it will need to be rewritten. I just want to expose you to the platform and let you pick which one resonates with you. Learn and master it, and once you think you've got it mastered, go back and learn again because platforms and technology change frequently. Learn, Implement, Master, Repeat.

If you're not comfortable with video, you can do a podcast where you just talk and don't have to be in front of a camera. If you don't like doing things like podcasts, you can write a blog. I could write an entire book on how to do these things correctly. Do a little research and find the medium you like best.

A Final Word on Social Media

To talk to your target market, you need to figure out what platform they're mostly on. So, if you're targeting millennials, you're going to be on SnapChat or Instagram as of right now. If you're targeting women between the ages of 29 to 35, you're going to be on Facebook. But because platforms, and technologies, and social media sites change so frequently, by the time this book is printed, that may have all changed! So, it's really important to stay on top of technology, and social media. Make sure you're researching and studying what's coming out and what's new.

> "But because platforms, and technologies, and social media sites change so frequently, by the time this book is printed, that may have all changed!"

Maybe you can see that your target market is on a few platforms. It would be great if you could do them all. However, if you try that, odds are you'll end up not doing any of them well. You need to pick the one that is most relevant to your potential client or customer. You need to stick with that platform. You need to just do it, and go for it, and master it. Once you've mastered it, and you're using it all the time, then you can add another. But please start with just one. You'll get the most traction and most success by doing just one really well.

Email

Whenever you ask for contact information, you are building your email list of potential customers and clients. A contact management system can help you keep track of contacts and sort them into subgroups for specialized marketing. But if you can't afford a contact management system, you can keep your contact list on an Excel spreadsheet to send out your marketing emails, or even better, use MailChimp. It's free. It can send out mass emails to your perspective clients then will let you know who is doing what (opening the email, deleting, following links, etc.) so you can respond appropriately. (MailChimp is a great software but you should do your own research to discover what software works best for you and your business.)

It's important that you build your contact list, so you can continue to market to leads you get from Facebook or LinkedIn ads. Because even though you're on these other platforms, like Facebook and YouTube, you don't own that platform. So if they were to ever disappear, you don't own that list. You want to develop your own list. You want to be able to get as many people on a list of email addresses and phone numbers. Then if anything happens to those portals, you're not left powerless. In order to do that, you need to be creating valuable content on a weekly basis that people give their contact information to get. You do this, so you can continue to future market to them and reach them.

The problem with email is that very few emails get opened. Think about it. What do you do when you first open your inbox? You skim down the list of new emails and hit delete, delete, delete, right? You might save certain things to look at later, but we all know what happens to those. They will sit in your inbox for a few weeks in the hopes that you'll have some free time to view them, then inevitably you delete those too. Or you might put an email in a folder with similar emails then forget it's there. More often than not, these just get deleted without being read also. We get so overwhelmed by the sheer volume of emails that even things that you thought might be important get deleted.

So, just be aware that regular emails are rarely opened. If you're going to market with email, you want to do video emails because video emails get opened way more often than regular emails. Video email is 90% more likely to be opened and a more effective to stay in touch with somebody. When compared to regular email, with video emails you get 81% more replies and you convert

68% more into customers. You get 56% more referrals, 87% more clicks, and 25% more double clicks using video email.

There are many effective ways to use email to connect with your target market. BombBomb is a video emailing software where you can send an actual video through an email. The video is moving, and you can even hold up a sign with the recipient's name on it. With a BombBomb video email, you can literally put someone's name on a small white board. For example, it could show up as "Hi, Nancy!" As Nancy is going through her email and she sees a live video with her name on a white board, she's going to open it, right?

I use a BombBomb video to follow up after meeting with a new or potential client. Doing something like sending a personalized video email or text message shows that you are going the extra mile. I've had clients say that receiving my video email was the one thing that made them finally realize, "Wow, this person is so on top of it. I want to work with her."

There are many different video emails you can do. You can do a thank you video email. You can do a request for a testimonial. You can do a "nice to meet you" or "thank you for the inquiry." You can do a video that says, "Hey, just wanted to say I'm thinking about you," or videos for anniversaries, birthdays, or congratulations. You can tell your client or customer what to expect during the process of working with you or how to use the product you just sent them. You can send a video email to encourage them. You can send a video based upon the specific action they took on one of your ads and retarget to them based upon the ad they were interested in.

If you were selling cookbooks, you could send a video email that says, "Thanks so much! Be sure to join my Facebook group, and make sure you take a picture of yourself with the book and tell me what your favorite recipe is."

A video email doesn't have to be personal. It can be a video email that's standard that goes out to everybody. But when they're seeing you, they're feeling that it's more personal.

Websites and Landing Pages

Websites are almost under-utilized now. A website is not nearly as important as your Facebook presence or the funnels and landing pages you create using Facebook or any of the other lead generation platforms you may be using already.

My own website is not used a whole lot. Instead I use landing pages. A landing page has a very specific product or piece of content. It's where you direct people to go when you market on Facebook or on LinkedIn. You direct them to go to this specific landing page and you give them exactly what it is that you want them to see. It's very easy to create and very inexpensive.

You can create a landing page directly in Facebook on your Ad Manager account. You can also create a landing page through Click Funnel.com using this bit.ly/KristaClickFunnel. I'm not just suggesting you use ClickFunnel because of my affiliate link. It really does work and it's helped me grow my business and helped many of my clients. Ontraport is another place to create landing pages and funnels.

The purpose of a landing page is to capture somebody's contact information. You create something of value then offer it free to people who fill out their contact information. It's a special offer, or an eBook, or a webinar, or anything of value you can give away. When you've created a landing page, you market it on Facebook (or use Facebook's own landing page) or whatever platforms you are using. People click on the link to the landing page and you're going to say, "Hey, click on this. I'm going to give you my free downloadable book. Just give me your email address and your name or your name, email address and phone number."

Once you have that contact information, you can use Click Funnel, Ontraport, MailChimp, or Infusionsoft (I call it Confusionsoft!) or any other kind of service to re-market to them. You continue to market to them, re-market to them and target them with specific free offerings and eventually sell them something. This is how you build up an email list.

Repurposing Videos

In the last chapter on videos, I mentioned that you can get a lot of different uses out of just one video. This will make more sense now that you're thinking about the platform you'll use. You want to be strategic when you repurpose a video so here's how we structure it. Once you have recorded a video, you take that video and get it transcribed using the captions option (rev.com). I use Rev.com. Having it transcribed gives you a written article or blog that you can post on your website or distribute in different ways. Of course, when you get your transcription, you have to go back and re-read it and edit out the ums and the ahs. Then you just format it, then copy and paste it with lots of emojis into your Facebook feed as well as your blog on your website. Even if you think your business is not appropriate for emojis (i.e. you're a tax accountant or an attorney), use them anyway! They make the user stop scrolling and take a look at your post or ad. It helps it look less like an ad and more like it's from a real person.

Use a lot of hashtags as well in all of your long scripts, posts or ads. It helps when people are looking for a certain subject. The more hashtags you have in every post the more likely your post is to be discovered. So now you've got two pieces of content: a video you can post and a transcription. You record a video and you upload it onto Facebook or whatever your main platform is. Next you take the transcription and upload the file into Facebook or the platform you're using so the transcription is on the bottom as your video plays. (Rev.com can get you the transcription in a Word file to upload directly into Facebook and YouTube.) Ten days after that, the transcription can go on your website as a blog. Next you upload that very same video onto YouTube about twenty days from the time you initially put the video on Facebook. On day thirty, you take the transcription of the words from the video and post onto Facebook in a long format (remember to use lots of emoji's). People don't even recognize it as the video you did.

> "The more hashtags you have in every post the more likely your post is to be discovered"

Next, you go through the transcription and pull out any inspiring or interesting quotes to create "quote cards." You simply place the quote on top of an image. You can make these for free with just a few clicks on a website called Canva.com. Post your quote cards at different times, maybe even two per day. For example, if in your video you said something really powerful like "Learn, implement, master, repeat," just make a quote card out of that with graphics or a background so that it stands out. Try to make your quote cards look the same to start establishing a brand that people begin to recognize. You can also take that same video and have an audio version created to give you little mini podcasts or even little mini inspirational quotes.

So literally from one video, you're repurposing it into all those other forms. You're getting a heck of a lot of mileage from the hour or so you spent making the video in the first place. And this applies to your podcasts and blogs as well. Anything you create can be re-used in different formats on different platforms.

SEO Search Engine Optimization

I do not claim to be an expert when it comes to SEO, but it is important that you get a general understanding of how SEO works and why it is so important. At some point, you may even want to bring an expert in to help you with SEO for your business.

In a nutshell, SEO is how people will find you on the internet. Think about it: Whenever you want a question answered, you plug specific words into Google or Yahoo. The search engine of these platforms then uses those words to *search* for what you're looking for. It comes up with pages of suggestions of sites or blogs or articles that might help you find the answer you're looking for.

In promoting your business, you want to be at the top (or close to the top) of those suggested sites or articles, right? Search engine optimization helps you get there.

First, the more articles, blogs and videos you post, the more likely someone's internet search will lead to you. You want to create content that is accurate, current and relevant. The search engines like Google rank your content in terms of how current it is. They will place your content closer to the top of their suggestions if it is more current. It's also important that your content is optimized to be mobile friendly. According to searchengineland.com, more than half of U.S. internet searches are now done on mobile devices. Google's algorithm also ranks your content higher if it is mobile friendly.

And keep in mind that your content is about serving, not selling. The secret to SEO is to give real value to your potential clients and customers. When people do a search, most often they are looking for answers or resources. Focus on creating content that truly answers the questions that keep them up at night and fills their needs. Think about why they are doing a search, what specific information they might be looking for, and how you can help them. How can you add value to their life, how can you serve them, how can you make their life easier?

> "When people do a search, most often they are looking for answers or resources. Focus on creating content that truly answers the questions that keep them up at night and fills their needs"

It's important to use proper "key" words or terms that the search engine can pick up. If you use words that are too broad, you'll probably end up at the bottom of the heap because zillions of items will show up. For example, when someone does a search for "Doctor in Brentwood California," the search engine will give you pages and pages of suggestions. But if you type in, "Doctors in Brentwood who specialize in asthma or rhinoplasty," the search engine will come up with many fewer suggestions. The odds of your being at the top of this list is much higher. So use proper key terms in your website and within the content you create. Don't be broad and general. Be as specific within your niche as possible. Make sure these good key words show up both in the title and in the body of your content, as well as all over your website. You can also use something like Rank Tracker to tell you if your content is fully optimized for specific keywords.

Also, be sure to title your content correctly. Think about the words someone will be typing into Google in their search. You would title something differently for Google than you would for Facebook. The title you post on Facebook is more to get someone to stop scrolling. However, when you create a title for YouTube or Google, your title should help someone find you when searching for that topic.

TAKE ACTION #18

Do some research about the top ten Google searches that come up regarding your product or service. Go to Google/BingWebmasterTools; Google Analytics; Keyword.io; AnswerThePublic.com Think about content you can create to elaborate and be more specific in answering questions people have. Check out a few of the top blogs or websites that the search engines suggest in your arena. What key words do they use?

We are barely touching on all of the tools you can use online to market yourself and your business. You've also got Google Adwords, doing display ads, banner ads, affiliate partnerships—the list goes on forever! Get started and do some research to see what fits you best.

CHAPTER 10

Finding Your Tribe

One of the most beneficial things you can do to market your business and keep the pipeline of customers and clients full is to create what we used to call "raving fans." These are people who are so impressed by you and your service that they are excited to tell all their friends about your business. And they are also the ones who are the most likely to buy the next thing you offer. Basically you want your tribe to be drinking your "Krista Juice" or product juice so to speak. You want them to have such an amazing experience with your product or service that they cannot help but tell the world.

According to InvespCro.com, "The probability of selling to an existing customer is 60 – 70%, while the probability of selling to a new prospect is just 5-20%." So keeping your customers and clients happy and close to you is incredibly important. Studies from Bain & Company as well as Harvard Business School claim that an increase of just 5% in customer retention will increase profits by 25% to 95%! Other studies show that existing customers are 50% more likely to try your new products. They also spend an average of 31% more than new customers.[6]

"

According to InvespCro.com, "The probability of selling to an existing customer is 60 – 70%, while the probability of selling to a new prospect is just

"

5-20%"

The internet has made it super easy to keep in touch with your customers and clients. It has also allowed businesses to take the raving fan idea even further to create "tribes" or fan clubs. Customers or clients who become members of your tribe get special attention and extra freebies, closer access to you, as well as value-added content that is created just for them.

Your tribe can become the blood of your business. Enthusiastic raving fans who would do anything for you (and you would do anything for them) is the basis of a tribe. You are creating an extended family. This is a place where people can go to be understood, to find people who are like them and understand their wants, desires, needs. It's a place where tribe members can be vulnerable and ask for help as well as give to others and serve. They get to interact with like-minded people, or people who are experiencing the same things they are experiencing in forums. They interact, they engage, and they help one another.

You need to really engage with people who become members as well. You want the members of your tribe to feel like they are part of something worth their time and valuable to their lives or their career. So you need to treat them that way and give them that value.

Just like you want your business to stand out and be different, you want your tribe to be different and unique as well. You want the tribe to reflect the unique personality of you and your business. It's okay for you to be different. You don't have to be like everyone else. When you are different, people in your tribe realize that this tribe is special. You always greet the tribe, talk to the tribe, and consider yourself a part of the tribe. You have a certain lingo that you use with them that is part of how you and your tribe are distinct from any other group.

Creating a Group

One really good way to set up a tribe is through a Facebook site. (You can do it through your own website, but you won't have all the tools you can get on Facebook.) Your Facebook group page and business page are similar but different. People who are interested in you and what you have to offer can become members of this group like any fan club. Initially, the group is public. But down the road, you may want to create a private group that gets extra perks. Creating a group and group page is free and Facebook will recommend your group to people who show behaviors and interests that match the group you create.

When someone joins your Facebook group, you can send them a video email about the rules of the group and the best ways for them to get engaged with the group. You can talk to them about the manifesto and purpose of the group. You can request that they do or don't do certain things. For example, when people buy my book, I say, "Hey, when you get the book, take a picture of yourself with it and post it in the group." That way they're engaging the group and they're promoting my book all at the same time.

Your group page is set up to be interactive with your members. They can post and comment on one another's posts. They can ask questions and give answers. They get to communicate with other people who are interested in what you have to offer, and they can develop relationships with each other.

> "If you're going to create a Facebook group, you have to be committed to being active in the group"

A Facebook group is one of the most powerful ways to engage your community. But here's the thing about a Facebook group: You have to monitor it. If you're going to create a Facebook group, you have to be committed to being active in the group. You have to be committed to giving value in the group. You have to be committed to responding to people, commenting, liking, sharing in their successes. You have to be committed to creating things within the group, so they are motivated to interact.

For example, you might say, "Tell me what your successes were today" or "Tell me what you're having problems with and need help with." You might ask members to give you their greatest hack for whatever your specific topic is, or you can ask them what they do on a daily basis to make their lives or businesses easier. You want to post things in the group that encourage people to interact and engage. And when they engage, you've got to engage back.

It's essential that you market your group broadly unless you already have a following. People have to know about the group to want to join it. If you already have a following, you can market to your following or email list and encourage them to join your group. If you really promote it and others promote it for you, your group can grow very large rather quickly. When I started my coaching business, I first targeted real estate agents. I created a business page then I created a group page that I initially called Krista Mashore Coaching.

Here is how I found members to join my group. I created a bunch of videos and ran them as target ads through my Ad Manager account. I started with 31 videos with specific tips to help real estate agents, like how to design effective flyers, connecting with clients with video emails, how to stay on top of the market, etc. When I first started running the ads, I didn't ask them to do anything. It was just a pure "give." I gave as much value as possible without asking them to take any action. I did this to give them a chance to get to know me and to see that I was the real deal prior to asking them to do anything. After running the ads to real estate agents for about a month, I started running different video ads and then included a link to my book, or to my Facebook group page.

My target community started to get to know me, like me and trust me. Then I started doing Facebook Lives, where twice a week I just gave content that was valuable to them. Sometimes, it was motivational tips on success and mindset. Sometimes, it was directly regarding real estate. Within a matter of a month, this group grew to a thousand people.

Initially, I paid Facebook to expose my group page to agents, so they would then want to join the group. You have to pay to play so to speak. I paid to get exposure and to be seen by people I didn't have direct access to. I made sure to give value and to let them know me. The more and more videos I sent out to my target market, not asking them for anything in return, but just giving value, the more they got to know, trust and like me. After time, I included a link to join my Seven Figure real estate coaching group. Eventually I ran ads for my first book to the people who had interacted with my videos by liking them, commenting or sharing them. This is the retargeting we talked about in Chapter 9.

The name of your group is really important. You need to think, "How is this going to help them?" It's never about you and how great you are, but about what benefit your audience will get. For example, when I first named my group, I used Krista Mashore Coaching. But no one knows what Krista Mashore Coaching is and they don't even know what business that relates to. So I changed it to Seven Figure Realtor Blueprint. Now they get the idea, "Hey, this is a seven-figure realtor group, and this is going to tell me how to be a seven-figure earner in real estate." As soon as I changed the name, the group grew exponentially very quickly.

Facebook Live

A great tool to use on your group page is Facebook Live. Facebook changes all the time so what's working now might not work in a week or in a day. But right now, everyone really likes Facebook Live. When you do a Live, members of your group are notified when you're going "live." They can see you live and can ask you questions directly.

When people join in to watch, you can see that they're joining in. Members can send you likes or comments. You always want to acknowledge them, mention their name and thank them for joining. And you always want to encourage them to ask questions and comment and share and like. You're developing a relationship with them and developing trust.

Doing a Facebook Live is as easy as using a cellphone. (Go onto Facebook to learn exactly how to do this.) If you have a cellphone, you just go on to your group page and you hit "Go Live." Then you create a fun title that is going to make people want to watch. Then you go live using your phone as your video camera. You can also use your laptop. You can also use an app called BeLive.tv to live stream your live video on Facebook. It's super easy and affordable. It's really cool because you can add borders, show comments that people post or choose to keep them hidden. You can add your branding colors and logo, so it makes it look more professional.

With Be Live TV, you can actually interview other people wherever they are and it's live. You give the person you'll be interviewing a link. They use that link to join you and you do a live interview that members of your group or your target market can see. You can interview anyone who might add value to whoever you're trying to market to. This is a feature of Facebook Live and can only be done live as of now.

Unlike other things you do, like videos and blogs which should be brief, a Facebook Live event needs to be at least 7 minutes long or so. It takes people time to sign on and you want to give them time to comment and ask questions. The more comments and the more likes and the hearts that you get, Facebook will organically push your Facebook Live. Stay on long enough to get people engaged and ask them to engage. People love to have their name mentioned. So anytime you see people signing on, be sure and say, "Hi, Jane, thanks for signing on." You want to say their names and encourage people to ask questions and comment throughout the time of your Facebook Live.

Get Personal

When people are in your group and on your Facebook Live, or touched by any part of your marketing, remember that people, your "tribe" want to get to know who you are. Everything doesn't have to be just business. They want to get to know you personally. They want to hear your successes. They want to hear your struggles. Vulnerability is one of the best ways to reach your target audience. When they see that you're vulnerable and that you're real, it puts you on their same playing level. As you start to develop this group and as you become the leader of the group, people might think you're out of reach or that they can't accomplish what you've accomplished. Go ahead and be vulnerable. Always try to end with a positive but it's okay to talk about some of your weaknesses or your struggles. It helps people get to see the real you.

> "Vulnerability is one of the best ways to reach your target audience. When they see that you're vulnerable and that you're real, it puts you on their same playing level"

A good example of this is a post I did in my own community. It was titled "A Confession and an Apology." And I had over 15,000 organic views on that and I received hundreds and hundreds of comments. It came about one day when I realized something about myself and was feeling a little vulnerable. I picked up my cell and recorded a video that said, "Hey, I want to apologize to my community. I'm a coach and a trainer but I haven't been coaching in my own community out of my own fear of lack and loss. I've been so afraid that if I gave away all my secrets to my direct competition, it would hurt me. Really, that's not what I teach or what I preach. I'm sorry and I'm going to change." I got an overwhelming number of responses, which led to several speaking engagements and live webinars.

By doing this and being vulnerable, not only was I practicing what I was preaching, but my reality was coming true. I was not operating with an abundant mindset and having that lack kept me from greater things. When I admitted to this fault, people just loved it.

The Modern Mom sometimes posts about a disastrous day she's just had. She talked about the day she peed her pants. She talked about some days that she doesn't want to get out of bed because she's just so exhausted. We've all been there, right? She personally says that the peeing her pants thing launched her career. Her most embarrassing moment was also her defining moment. It propelled her from being nobody to being a star because they saw her vulnerability and her realness. It really set her career on fire.

I'm not saying by any means to be fake or make up that stuff. Just be real with people and don't be afraid to let people see who you really are. I used to think, "No one cares. No one wants to know about me." But people really do care and want to know. As you start to become a leader, as you start to inspire people, as you start to help people, as you start to be respected, they want to know about you. They want to learn about you and hear from you.

You as Tribe Leader

It's really important, especially when you're starting out, that you're a really strong leader in your tribe. You want to create ground rules and a manifesto that talks about the purpose of your tribe. This is like any group and can get a little weird if you don't set it up properly. You can request that members do not do certain things, for instance self-promotion or promotion of other groups or organizations. Insisting that your group is drama-free and a place to uplift one another is also a must. People need to feel safe in your group and in the tribe in which you created. You want people to have a positive experience in the group.

> "People need to feel safe in your group and in the tribe in which you created. You want people to have a positive experience in the group"

One tribe I know of has the rule that there are no political or religious discussions or postings about those topics allowed on the group page. When people post things like that, it often stirs up arguments. So if someone posts something political or about religion, the leader of the group will give them a warning. If they do it again, they are kicked out of the group. It sounds harsh, but you'd be surprised how sour a group can turn from just one member who stirs things up like that.

You need to listen to your tribe. You have to pay attention to what your tribe is interested in and what they are posting. When you do this, you will understand their concerns and desires, and you'll know how to address them.

You need to be available to your tribe. You can't just whip up content and push it out then disappear. You need to actively engage in what you're posting and how they're responding to it. If you walk away, so will your tribe. The more you engage and are present, the more you'll reap the benefits from the time and energy you put in.

You need to take a stand about who and what you're about. Your tribe should have its own unique character that can be distinguished from other groups. You need to be laser-focused. Your tribe should be a specific niche, a specialty, not just a jack of all trades master of none.

You need to provide great quality. It's better to do less and do it consistently well, rather than producing huge quantities of half-baked content in sporadic bursts.

Your tribe needs to be the right size, so you can give them attention. You're better off -and will make more money—if you have 1,000 devoted followers who buy everything you offer than if you have 10,000 members who aren't fully participating in the tribe because you haven't been able to engage with them. If your tribe gets too large, you can create "Elite" tribes for paying members who then get more of your focus.

You need to be consistent and patient. Your tribe will not grow overnight. It takes time and continuous effort on your part. The longer you build and the more value you give, people will be inspired to refer you to their friends.

You need to expose your tribe to other experts and influencers. Interview other professionals in similar businesses who can offer value to your tribe. You need to constantly build relationships with other leaders. You never know how someone may be able to help you. Offering content of value to someone with lot of followers and who is an influencer can help both of you. They get to bring additional value to their tribe and you get in front of new audiences. Who are the online influencers in your market who have a quality audience that might be interested in what you have to offer? Research your competitors or people in a similar space as you. Connect and build relationships with these people. Show interest in them, comment, like, and share their posts. Add value if you are in their groups. As they notice you, they may share and push you and your content out to their tribes.

You need to stay active in your group, respond to posts and messages, offer answers to questions and possible solutions to problems. Building the relationship is one of the most important parts of a tribe's success. Acknowledge all who join and reach out to you.

"Building the relationship is one of the most important parts of a tribe's success"

You need to be grateful and appreciative. Be thankful for your tribe and make sure they know it. Don't ever take the power and support of your tribe for granted. Make sure you let them know how important they are to you and to the community as a whole often.

You want a tribe and a place for your people to go so you can add as much value to their life as possible. Here is where you want to give all of your stuff away. I know you're freaking out about "giving it all away." As I have said close to ten thousand times already, the more you give the more you'll attract the people who want more of what you have to offer. They will buy your products because they know it will help change their life. They will buy from you because they trust you and your goods and services. Your tribe will save you money because these people already respect you and your goods or service. This is your golden ticket and nugget. Don't take it lightly. Respect and nurture it and the rewards will be endless.

To end this book, I'd like to leave you with my personal keys to success. I've learned these from many of the great coaches and teachers I've had over the years as well as from some amazing books I've read. I've applied them in my own life and can honestly tell you they work. I put these keys together based on the letters of Believe U Can—with a couple of extras thrown in!

Believe: To succeed at this or just about anything in life, you need to get your head straight and keep it straight. This means noticing when your thoughts wander into negativity and cutting them off at the pass. This means infusing your brain with positive teachings from teachers like Napoleon Hill or Dale Carnegie. This means not buying into your self-doubts or letting any negative circumstance determine your attitude. You get what you think about. Think and know that you can do or be anything that you want to. You are the only person that can get you there or who can stop you from getting there. My new favorite book is *You Are A Badass* by Jen Sincero. The tagline is *How to Stop Doubting Your Greatness and Start Living an Awesome Life*. She teaches that you can do anything no matter what it is, but you need to believe it. The book is very similar to *Think and Grow Rich* but a little easier to understand (especially for teens). Also, *The Five Second Rule* by Mel Robbins is a book that will help you reach your goals, achieve anything you desire and overcome any obstacle you may be experiencing.

There is one quality which one must possess to win, and that is definiteness of purpose, the knowledge of what one wants, and a burning desire to possess it.

— Napoleon Hill

Educate: Be an educator, not a self-promoter. First become a true expert then share your expertise. Give people in your community information that will keep them abreast of what's happening. Give your clients information that will help them make good decisions. Be the go-to person for anyone who wants to know about your market. Show your community all the knowledge you have, share it with them. This is what sets you up to be seen as a leader.

Education is for improving the lives of others and for leaving your community and the world better than you found it.

— Marian Wright Edelman

Learn: To educate others, you first have to learn enough to be a true expert—and keep learning. Tap the knowledge of mentors and coaches. Study critical areas of your business. Improve in areas where you're weak by taking classes, webinars and workshops. Learning should never stop, we need to constantly learn, improve and add to our piggy bank of knowledge.

An investment in knowledge pays the best interest.

— Benjamin Franklin

Innovate: Be different! Stay in the mode of creating new ways of doing things. Use technology to reach more people, be more efficient, and get better results. Don't stick with "the ways we've always done it." Find new, better, more efficient ways of doing everything and never stop doing this. When everyone else is doing ABÇ, you do PDQ and do it with a BANG!!

If you always do what you've always done, you'll always get what you've always gotten.

— Mark Twain, Henry Ford, Tony Robbins

Engage/Everywhere: Engage your community by offering them valuable information that is relevant to them. Engage them by using video so they can feel a more personal connection. Be everywhere using social media and the internet with your informational videos, ads and listings. Let people know you before they meet you. Get personal with them. You'll see how powerful this is and how quickly you'll see the results. Engagement is equal to connection and connection is so powerful. Think about the dynamics with your family and friends. You've built a strong connection that keeps you close. This will help you to earn trust, respect and be looked upon as a leader.

Communication - the human connection - is the key to personal and career success.

— Paul J. Meyer

Value: Give real value in everything you do. Go so far above and beyond for your clients and customers that they are thrilled to pay you. Constantly ask, "What more can I do to serve?" People are mainly concerned with themselves and what you can do for them. How can you help them? What's in it for them? Always focus on what you can give them. Also, stick to your own values and be impeccably ethical in all you do.

Great salespeople are relationship builders who provide value and help their customers win.

— Jeffrey Gitomer

Energy/Enthusiasm: Love what you do! Tackle every project, every class, every interaction as if it's your favorite thing to do. Show up with confidence that you'll do an outstanding job. Answer the phone with a smile. Show the world that you love life, you love them, and you love what you do!

Flaming enthusiasm, backed up by horse sense and persistence, is the quality that most frequently makes for success.

— Dale Carnegie

Unique: Seek to stand out from the crowd and be different in all you do. Capitalize on your gifts, share them with the world. Being unique is what makes you memorable. If you do things like everyone else, you'll blend in and get lost in the shuffle. Successful people don't just blend in with the crowd. Your unique personal qualities and business practices will help you lead in your field.

You are unique, and if that is not fulfilled, then something has been lost.

— Martha Graham

Courageous: Be bold and persistent. Do whatever it takes to serve your clients and customers and to reach your goals, even if it scares the heck out of you. Take each failure, learn what it can teach you, then try again. Your dreams are totally attainable. They just need a timeline and a series of smaller goals attached to them. Right now, I am pursuing my dream. I have to tell you, by doing this I am truly happier now than I've ever been I feel so content and satisfied. I'm generally a very happy person, but it's now at a different level. I am happier in my marriage than ever before, and in my relationships with my children, friends and peers. When you're bold enough to go after your dreams and what inspires you, it makes you show up differently in life.

All our dreams can come true if we have the courage to pursue them.

— Walt Disney

Articulate/Action: Learn to express yourself to your community and your clients. Communicate clearly and with patience, remembering that others don't have your expertise. Articulate your appreciation. And take action! Make a plan to achieve your goals and act on that plan. Be sure to implement what you learn. Work it, tweak it, adjust what you are doing and keep making it better and better. If you learn something and it doesn't work, that's okay. You will fail a few times, but get back up and eventually, you'll find something that is a home run.

Create a definite plan for carrying out your desire and begin at once, whether you are ready or not, to put this plan into action.

— Napoleon Hill

Niche: Don't try to be everything to everyone. Focus your business on the niche that fits you the best. Learn what you need to learn to succeed in that niche. You don't have to be all things to all people. Look at what you enjoy, what you want to specialize in and be laser focused on that. Perfect that one area and capitalize on it.

Identify your niche and dominate it. And when I say dominate, I just mean work harder than anyone else could possibly work at it.

— Nate Parker

Two final keys: Gratitude and Persistence: I am a big believer in the power of gratitude. Now research has shown that gratitude is not just something for Sunday school or people who have watched *The Secret*. A recent Harvard Medical School article said, ". . .gratitude is strongly and consistently associated with greater happiness. Gratitude helps people feel more positive emotions, relish good experiences, improve their health, deal with adversity, and build strong relationships."

We get caught up in pursuing our goals and wanting to be better, more prosperous and successful. There's nothing wrong with that. However, while we're doing that, it's important to be grateful for what you already have and who you already are— everything in your life. Even if you're struggling financially, odds are that you have more than 93% of the world's population. And more importantly, you have the opportunities to turn that around. Be grateful for that.

Be grateful that you ran into this book. I've offered you so many tools that will truly make a difference in your business and your life. Treat the knowledge I've shared as the gift it is and take action on it. Be grateful for whatever level of health, prosperity and community connections you have.

Take nothing for granted—your family, your friends, your opportunities, your well-being. Appreciate the life you've been given and all that you've experienced. If you feel inclined to whine and complain about something, knock it off! Wallowing in regrets or "if only's" never got anyone anywhere. Step into the attitude of gratitude and notice what a difference it makes.

When you look for what's working in your life, it expands.

— Marchall Sylver

Wishing you the very best in life!

www.ingramcontent.com/pod-product-compliance
Lightning Source LLC
LaVergne TN
LVHW022054200926
848481LV00003B/900
* 9 7 8 1 8 0 7 6 5 0 8 2 7 *